Worm Farm

Worm Farming Guide

Worm farming costs, care, housing, feeding and how to start a worm farm business.

By

Tori Luckhurst

CW00549291

Table of Contents

Chapter 1. Introduction to Worm Farming

Worm farming is the last thing many people will consider. A lot of people out there don't even know that certain species of worms can be farmed, harvested and sold for profit. They can also be farmed for study purposes or for fun. The truth is that the farming of worms, especially as a part of organic natural gardening methods, is growing in popularity. It is technically called vermicomposting or vermiculture. I have been into worm farming for many years. I farm worms not just as hobby but also as a source of revenue. It is also a good means through which I manage my organic waste. You or your kid may have interest in worm farming and that is why you are reading this book now.

I am going to share my many years of experience as a worm farmer with you. Indeed, worm farming is interesting and rewarding. But despite its numerous advantages, it has some drawbacks. Let me begin with the ugly side of this wonderful leisure and economic activity.

The Dark side of Worm Farming

You may be wondering why I prefer to start with the disadvantages of worm farming. It is not to frighten you or discourage you from having a worm farm. Instead, it is to immediately let you know the risk you run in order to motivate you and inspire you to take the bull by the horns. Besides, it will help you to resolve on time whether or not to move into it. So, before going into this type of composting, first take time to know the risks involved in it.

First, it can be an easy means of contacting bacterial infections, especially when it is being managed by children. Disease-causing bacteria may be present in the compost and the soil. They can enter into the body through tears and cuts on the skin. So, if you have any cuts or your child has, it is advisable that you avoid coming to your worm farm until you are completely healed. It is also based on this reason that I strongly recommend that you put on gloves and a nice pair of garden shoes or any other suitable pair of shoes when you are working or doing anything in your worm farm to reduce the risk of getting infections. Ensure that you wash your hands and, if possible, take a shower after spending some time in your worm farm. I will advise schools that have worm farms for teaching and experiment purposes to provide gloves for their students and ensure that they put them on whenever they are in the garden.

Worm farms normally attract fruit flies and other insects, especially if they are poorly managed. With odour oozing out from a dirty and poorly kept worm compost,k it is easy to see why this problem occurs. Besides, these flies are looking for food. They want to take their own share of the crumbs. As the flies are feasting on your worm foods, they also lay their eggs there and begin to multiple. When they eventually increase in number, your farm will gradually be filled with flies. This was a very big challenge to me when I started worm farming for the first time. However, I later developed a good strategy of dealing with the problem. All you have to do is to conceal the food scraps from the flies and to ensure that your worm farm does not have any odour.

Normally, flies do not burrow. But worms do. I do bury my worms' food under the castings and bedding. The worms will find the food there while the flies will not be able to find them. It is also good if you wrap their food in newspapers. They can pierce through it. Make the top of your compost's bedding damp to make it difficult for flies to survive there. But it should not be to the detriment of your worms. I will tell you more about this in the chapter that deals with worm housing requirements. Another veritable means of getting rid of flies is to set trap for them. A mixture of milk saucer, apple cider vinegar and a drop of dish soap is a good trap for flies. Prepare your trap and keep it close to your vermipod.

When a few factors in worm farming like overfeeding the worms goes wrong, your vermicompost can become malodorous. The University of Nebraska Extension has also highlighted the possibility of a worm's bin developing an earthy odour. But it is possible to reduce the possibility of your worm farm producing an offensive stench by doing what's neccesary. First, don't over feed your worms. If the worms have too much food that they cannot consume it all, the scraps will decay and this will cause your vermipod to become smelly. Providing them with wet food also creates the problem of odour. Another means of preventing your worm farm from becoming malodorous is to ensure that your worm bin has adequate air circulation. But note that it is almost impossible to make a worm farm completely odourless. You can reduce the odour to a level where it will not constitute any discomfort to your household or people living within the same compound and neighbourhood with you.

Worm farming is time consuming and also somewhat expensive to manage. Being expensive here is much more than money. First, it is not a good means of managing a large quantity of organic waste. If you go into it with the purpose of managing your waste and you generate a huge quantity of waste in your home over a short period of time, you will definitely become disappointed when your worms die. Worm farms require low temperatures for waste to decompose unlike the traditional form of composting that requires high temperatures. If you mistakenly provide a huge amount of waste in your vermicompost bin within a short period of time, your worms are likely to die because the temperature will increase and the compost will become unfavourable for their survival.

Worms becomes dehydrated in an environment with a high temperature and this will cause their untimely death. If you want to process large amounts of waste, then you have to get a number of bins and split them among the bins so that you will not heap organic waste in a bin which can cause the mercury to go up to a level that will be detrimental to your worms. You may also consider combining traditional composting and vermicomposting to handle your large waste. But this will also add to your work load.

Worm farming also needs more care when compared to the traditional composting. To ensure that the worms are healthy, you have to provide them with the right quantity of food, so that their living environment will be suitable for their survival. Again, you will require special species of worms. As we shall discuss later, it is not every type of worm that can be farmed.
Vermicomposting/vermiculture also requires special metal or plastic containers. You will have to balance the acid levels generated by the waste in the new soil with lime. Above all, worms eat a lot. Every

worm eats up to half of their weight. You may spend a reasonable amount of money for their feeding especially if you don't generate a large quantity of waste.

Large scale worm farming also needs a lot of space. In order to ensure that your farm gives a large yield as traditional compost, you will have many worm bins and these will take up some space in your yard or garden. Thus, if you have limited space, you may not be able to go into large scale worm farming. Worm composting does not terminate weeds and pathogens. This is because it requires a low temperature. This environment favours the survival of these weeds and microorganisms. Pests like centipedes also survive in vermicompost. Thus, owning a worm farm is tantamount to sending out an invitation to these pests and pathogens.

It is labour intensive to harvest worms or take out the fertile soil or manure built up in vermicompost. This is because you have to separate the worms from the soil which can be very challenging and time consuming depending on the number of worms farmed and the number of bins that you have. But, this problem does not occur in traditional composting.

Note that vermiculture and vermicompost (worm growing and worm compost) do not necessarily work well together. This means that if you are growing worms, you will not get enough casting from your worms to sell. Similarly, if you are into worm composting, your worm farm will not produce enough worms for you to sell. This is because of the difference in the way their beddings are prepared and the different ways they are managed. For example, if you are growing worms, you don't have to wait for your worms to turn almost all the beddings into cast before you can harvest. You can harvest when there are more worms in the bin. Constantly splitting worms to ensure that they keep procreating can affect the quantity of cash they will produce (I shall explain this in details later in this book). But you can also combine and excel in both if you know what you are doing.

Why We Should All Be Worm Farmers
Despite the various disadvantages and the risks posed by worm farming, there are still strong reasons why I think it is worth going

into. In fact, the advantages of worm farming outweigh its disadvantages. It is a type of farming that benefits not just the farmer but also the entire ecosystem. Here are various reasons why families, individuals, farmers and educational institutions should consider owning worm farms.

Affordable means of managing waste
Worm farming is an affordable means of managing organic waste, food scraps and kitchen waste. Rather than sending your organic waste to the landfills and get them quickly filled, you can manage them by yourself from your home. Depending on the size of your worm farm, all your kitchen waste can go into it. Vermicomposting/vermiculture is a great service to the entire nations and the world at large. Indeed, we generate huge quantities of organic waste from our various homes on daily basis. The landfill easily gets filled up. The government of every country spends a huge amount of money in the management of waste in the landfill. But a lot can be saved if at least 20 percent of the population of a country has this type of compost in their gardens.

With the amount of waste that goes into the landfill on yearly basis, untold harm is done to our ecosystem. Our streams, rivers and oceans are polluted by the leachate produced in landfill. Large amounts of green gases that destroy the ozone layers which yield us from the scorching effect of the UV rays from the sun are generated from the landfill. By having a worm farm, you contribute to reducing these environmental problems caused by landfills. With lesser quantities of waste going into the landfill, the amount of leachate and green gases generated there will reduce drastically. In sum, establishing your worm farm is a good means of going green or imbibing an eco-friendly lifestyle.

A great way of improving the quality of agricultural soil
Worms burrow in the soil. Some species dig deep into the soil while some could only dig a few inches below the top soil. Regardless of how deep or shallow their tunnels are, their actions enhance air and water circulation in the soil which is very beneficial to the farmers. Crops, plants and trees grow well where the soil is well aerated with more water coming in.

Again, worms in the farm produce vermicast which is a juice-like substance that is very rich in plant foods and minerals. If you have a garden or a farm, you can apply the vermicast produced in your worm farm there as a natural fertiliser. Thus, it will save you the cost of purchasing artificially made fertilizers for your plants. It has also been established through research that worms help in stabilising the soil pH level. The vermicast produced by worms has a neutral pH level of close to 7.

This means that they are not acidic or alkaline in nature. Many plants do well in a soil with a pH level that is 7 or a little bit below or above this number. It is because of the agricultural benefits of worms that made Charles Darwin, the great evolutionist, to denominate them as "Nature Plough." With worm casting, your vegetables will get enough nourishment, grow bigger and taste better. You can also use it to grow your flowers.

Feeding worms and management of worm farms are not complicated tasks that can be handled by adults only. Children can also handle them. In fact, it is a task that most children will like to do. Thus, if you have kids, you can keep your worms in their care insofar as you take note of the risk factors mentioned above and provide adequate protection to them. Allowing children to manage worm farms is a good means of boosting their sense of responsibility for their actions. It teaches them the importance of recycling and the need to save our environment from decay. It will help them to learn how to live an eco-friendly life style. With a worm farm in your garden, you are giving your children the opportunity of having a practical experience of what they learn about ants in their various schools.

Last but not the least, worm farming is a good source of income. As I mentioned above, I farm worms not just as a pastime activity but also to make money. After fattening and growing large numbers of worms, I sell them to make money. I will tell you more about the worm business in detail in the last chapter of this book. For now, bear in mind that you will reap the fruit of your labour at last if you are very careful about it.

Difference between Worm Farming and Composting

Worm farming, also known as vermiculture, is very similar to composting. Many people use the two terms interchangeably without knowing that they are not same. Worm farming is indeed quite different from traditional composting in a number of ways and the two terms should not be used interchangeably, regardless of their close similarities. Composting is best suited for managing large quantities of waste. A compost bin can contain large quantities of organic waste which makes their temperature very high.

It is a slower method of processing waste. In other words, a composting bin can be described as a hot system with large capacity for a slow processing of organic waste. Compost bins are the best means of processing certain waste such as citrus, cabbage, onion, lawn clippings and others.

Worm farming on the other is a process of breeding worms for commercial purposes. The vermipod or bin used for worm farming here is small in size. Thus, a worm farmer requires many of them in order to produce a large number of worms simultaneously. Due to the differences between these two methods of composting, they do not have the same advantages and disadvantages but their end result is the same. In composting, there are no worms to sell, pathogens to fear and no weed because of the high heat environment. But it takes a longer time to process waste with this system when compared with vermiculture. While worm farming gives quicker returns and can be turned into a money making business, it is more stressful to manage and expose owners to the risk of contracting infections.

Vermiculture and Vermicomposting

Many people also use vermiculture and vermicomposting interchangeably, thinking that they are the same. The two terms are very similar in meaning. In practice, the difference between them is very subtle because the goal of one can be realized through the other. In vermiculture, worms are bred to be sold. But in the process of breeding worms, organic waste is processed and turned into manure, though in little quantity when compared with worm composting. Thus, the little castings produced can also be sold. Vermicomposting on the other hand refers to a cool composting system utilized for quick processing of organic waste. In this method of waste processing, worms are utilised to process organic matter into humus. The objective is to produce worm casting. But in the process, worms are fattened and populated even though the population is controlled. Both the worm and the casting can be sold. You can see for yourself why it is difficult to differentiate between these two terms.

Chapter 2. Worms at a Glance

Worm is a general name for any invertebrate animal which has no limb but has a long, soft and slender body. They are available in different classes, namely, segmented worms (Phyla Annelida), roundworms (Nematoda) and flatworms. Here, we are concentrating more on phylum Annelida, which is tube-shaped. Earthworms normally live in the soil where they obtain their nourishment from dead or live organic material. They are available in different species. But all worms have a similar nature and thus, their anatomies are the same. In this chapter, I am going tell you a little bit about the bodily structure of earthworms, their life cycle and available species. If you are planning to set up a worm farm, it is important that you know about the anatomy of worms as this will help you to distinguish your earthworms and species of earthworms that can be farmed from other types of worms that cannot be farmed.

Anatomy of Worms

Earthworms vary in dimension. The adult worms of this class are within the range of 10mm (0.39in) L x 1mm (0.039 in) W to 3m (9.8 ft.)L x 25mm (0.98)W. Mantas mekongianus, which is the longest known species of earthworm, is about 3m long. They are found along Mekong River's banks in Southeast Asia. Generally, earthworms are cylindrical in shape. They are segmented. The segments are referred to as metamerisms. The body has furrows, which are a type of visible grooves that distinguish the segments. On each of the segments are bristle-like hairs known as lateral setae, which provide support to the body of the worms when they are moving. Worms also have special kinds of ventral setae that provide support to mating earthworms. The number of setae available in an earthworm depends on it species. There are some species that have four pairs and some that have over eight pairs. Worms from birth already get all the setae it will have throughout its life cycle.

In general, the mouth and anal segments have not got these lateral setae. The first segment contains the mouth and prostomium which is a fleshy lobe that overhangs the mouth. The prostomium plays a couple of roles in worms. First, worms use it to feel and sense their environment. Second, when they are at rest, they also use this part of the first segment to seal the entrance. In certain species of earthworms, the prostomium is prehensile. With it, they can grab and pull things inside their living tunnels. There is a raised band that surrounds a number of segments available in the front part of worms. Called the clitellum, this belt-like glandular swelling comprises the reproductive segments of earthworms. It produces egg capsules. The posterior part of worms is cylindrical in shape. However, there are some species that are trapezoidal, octagonal, flattened or posterior. The last segment, which contains the anus is called the periproct. The anus has a vertical but short opening.

Worm do not breathe through the mouth, instead, it breathes through the dorsal pores and nephridiopores. Fluid that protects the worms' surface or exterior and provides it with moisture comes out from these pores. A thin cuticle is located on the exterior of each individual segment over the skin. Its colour ranges from red to brown. This part of the body features certain cells that produce and deliver mucus through the cuticle to the exterior body in order to moisten it and make movement through the soil easier. Worms have two layers of muscles and a layer of nerve tissue under their skin.

The coelom, which is a chamber filled with fluid, is situated interior to this layer of muscles. This chamber gives earthworms their body shape through a process of self-pressurization. The septum (called septa in plural form) demarcates the segments from each other. They are perforated, transverse dividing walls which make it possible for the fluid coming from the coelom to get through the segments. At the rear of a septum is a pair of structures known as nephrostomes. Each nephrostome has a nephric tubule that goes into the next segment to the nephridum or metanephridium through the septum. The nephridum or metanephridium is the name for the organ of the body that detoxifies the coelomic fluid pushing out all unwanted materials through nephridiopores at the sides of the body of a worm. Most of the segments have two or more of these pores. When stressed, certain species of earthworm, such as the blue squirter earthworm, (scientifically known as Didymogaster Sylvaticus) eject fluid from the coelom via the pores on their back.

The digestive tract of worms is centrally located and goes from the mouth to the anus. Though it is flanked above and below the blood vessels and ventral nerve cord, it does not coil at any point. A pair of pallial blood vessels surrounds the digestive tract.

Just like various kinds of living things, earthworms also have different systems, with each consisting of different organs. The major systems of an earthworm include the central nervous system, peripheral nervous system, sympathetic nervous system, digestive system, reproductive system, circulatory system and excretory system. Among all these systems of earth worms, I am going to talk about the reproductive organs. I consider this system very important for the type of project you are planning to undertake – worm farming. This does not mean that other systems are not important. But it is important that you know how your worms populate and perpetuate their kinds.

Reproductive system of worms

Earthworms, like other kinds of worms, are hermaphrodites meaning that each worm is both male and female. The male and female sexual organs are available in the 9 to 15 segments of each worm. The seminal vesicles, where sperm are produced are cream coloured and situated towards the worm's anterior. During mating, sperm is released from this organ through the male pores from the 15th segment. The female reproductive organ, namely, the oviducts and ovaries, where the eggs are produced are contained in the 13th segment. The eggs are released from here through the female pores on the 14th segment.

During copulation, each mating adult provides both the sperms. The sperm from a mating partner enters the spermathecae which are available in 9th and 10th segment. They are stored and preserved there. In other words, sperm cells are released from segment 15 from one partner into the segment 9 and 10 of the other mating partner. There are some species of worms that transfer sperms via external spermatophores.

A worm ready to mate attracts a partner through chemical signalling, with pheromones playing an active role here. The partners overlap front ends ventrally in order to copulate. After the release and transfer of sperm, they disintegrate. Long after they have disintegrated, the clittelum of each of the mated worm will secrete a substance that will turn into a ring around the worm. This ring-like substance contains the eggs. As the worm moves about, the ring will pull out from the body and seals to form the cocoon where the egg will hatch. Note that in some species, the mated worm will transfer both the sperm it receives from the mating partner and her own eggs into the ring as the ring is about to slide off from the body. A new worm will be formed which will also get out of the ring. But the embryonic earthworm still needs to develop into fully fledge adult. The cocoon ends will seal to form a natural incubator which is lemon-like in shape. It is within this cocoon that baby worms will develop.

At the completion of the incubation period, the baby earthworm will come out fully developed. But it is still tiny. It will require about 60 to 90 days to become a fully sized adult worm depending on the species you have. Some species will require longer time to mature.

Regeneration

Another important aspect of perpetuation of kinds in worm is their ability to regenerate lost parts or segments. It has been discovered through research, especially that carried out by G.E Gates over twenty years ago, that worsm can regenerate themselves. If you cut a worm in two, each half will continue its independent existence and will regenerate into a complete adult with all the organs and systems of worms. However, it is the severity and extent of damage that will determine whether this ability will be actualized or not. I have to warn you immediately here, don't attempt to increase the number of your worms by cutting them into two unless you are ready to bear the loss if you end up killing them.

No scientific study has conclusively proved regeneration ability of worms as a practical means of populating them. But on the level of theory it has been proven. Besides, the regeneration ability differs from species to species. To learn more about regeneration, you should take time read more about Gates' study.

Now, let us discuss the lifecycle of a worm from fertilization to adult stage till death.

Life Cycle of Worms

Worms pass through four stages before death which include the egg, baby, adult and reproductive stage. At each of these stages, they exhibit a certain form of characteristics. Below are basic characteristics of each stage.

Egg stage

Earthworms could be regarded as oviparous animals, even though they do not lay eggs in the same manner with most other oviparous animals. As evident from above, every earthworm begins life inside an egg cocoon when the male sperm fertilizes the female egg. During the incubation period, which will last about three week or more depending on the species, it will undergo several transformative changes to hatch into baby worms with each being about ½ an inch depending on the species. It is also possible for a cocoon to stay for years before hatching. It can only hatch when there is a favourable condition for that. The right condition includes the right weather and right soil.

Put differently, the incubation period of a cocoon depends on a number of factors, which include the type of species, weather conditions and soil type. So, earthworm's incubation period is not a given. But if the weather and soil are ok, you should expect your cocoon to start hatching within three weeks to five. A cocoon normally contains more than one baby worm. In some species, the number may be up to 20 while in some others it may be less or more.

Baby worm

A baby worm resembles an adult worm in all aspects except in size and colour, plus it does not have any reproductive organs. In colour, it is whitish but as they fend for themselves and struggle to survive, their colour gradually changes to the normal colour of an adult worm of their species. Just like certain reptiles and amphibians, mother worms don't take care of their babies. They start independent existence from the moment they are hatched. They will start eating immediately. A baby worm will be about ½ an inch depending on the species. Under the right conditions and with good nourishment, they are likely to grow into full adults within a month and half or more, depending on the species.

Adult stage

It is at this stage that their reproductive organs become well developed and matured. They can use them for procreation, the process of which I have briefly explained above. The lifespan of an adult worm is about 10 years in some species. There are some species that have a longer lifespan and those with a shorter lifespan. However, when they are farmed, they tend to live a shorter life. I cannot actually tell you from experience how long they can live in the farm because I do harvest and sell them when they grow in population. But some literatures have it that while held in captivity, they will live about two years. Adult earthworms are available in different colours. There are red, brown, green and blue coloured earthworms.

The reproduction stage

This is the final stage in the life cycle of worms. I have already explained the reproductive process of worms above. The process will continue till death and when baby worms become adults, they will continue the process.

Species of Worms

There are worms in all parts of the world. You will find at least one known species of worm in every continent. There are more than 3,000 thousand worm species world over. Unfortunately, not every species of earthworm can be farmed. So, it is good that you know the species that can be farmed. But this is a difficult task, given the availability of plenty species of worms. We can make this easy by classifying the species into various classes according to their habitat and feeding manner as well as basic characteristics. Later in chapter 4, I am going to tell you which species is the best to farm.

Classification based on nutrition and habitat
Compost worms

Also called Epigeic, Compost worms are earthworms belonging to the family of Oligochaeta. They play an important role in horticultural and agricultural systems. The major distinguishing aspect of the worm is where they make their feeding manner and habitat. They normally don't burrow deep inside the soil. Their tunnels are just about 12cm from the topsoil. They feed on decaying vegetable matter on top soil. They also search for foods on the rhizosphere of plant roots. They are not seen in the normal garden, but can be seen in leaf piles and manure heaps as they forage for food. Bacteria and fungi normally do no harm to them. They are like spices for garnishing foods.

Another distinguishing characteristic of this kind of worm is that they don't maintain a permanent habitat, rather they prefer burrowing here and down on decaying matter and topsoil. However, during cold weather or extreme hot weather, they create deeper holes and coil up secreting slime to cover themselves with so that they will not dry out. During this period, they go into hibernation.

Generally, they are small in size with an adult worm having a length of about 1 to 7 cm. Their colour varies from red to brown. Their back and head are darker in colour than any other parts. The reason for their pigmentation in the thinking of some scientists is to protect them from UV rays from the sun and other predators. Four main species of compost worms are Eisenia fetida, dendrobaena venta, lumbricus rubellus and Eisenia Andrei. Each of these species has its unique characteristics despite exhibiting the general characteristics of the class.

The earth worker worms

This class of earthworm is typically found in the garden and farms. In fact, they are called earth workers because of their efficiency in making vertical tunnels in the earth, which enhances air and water circulation on the soil. Their tunnels are about 50cm feet deep inside the earth. They cover the entrance of their burrows with their cast and leaves with certain shapes. They feed on soil and some types of leaves. They normally search for their food during the night time. Charles Darwin, popularly known for the evolution theory, studied these species of worm and it is most likely that they were the species he referred to as the nature ploughs.

They are called endogenic worms because they live inside the earth. They create permanent tunnels unlike compost worms. They are not pigmented and thus can be whitish, yellowish, grey-bluish or pinkish in colour. They may appear to be dark in colour if they fill their gut with dark soil. But, you should not confuse them with epigeic species because their head and back have not got the red-brown skin pigmentation which both the epigeic and anecic species have. Their length varies between 2 and 12cm depending on the species. Typical examples of species of worms that belong to this group are Octolsion tyrtaeum, Aporrectodea species and Octolasion cyaneum.

Root dwelling worm/deep burrowing species

As implicit from the name, this type of worm dwells under the root of plants and trees where they will feed on fungi and decaying roots as well as on fresh surface litter which they drag inside their burrow. They are mostly available in areas with vegetation and farmlands. But unlike earth workers, which can be seen around in the farm, you cannot easily see this type of worm on the earth's surface.

They spend more of their life underneath the plant root where they feed and procreate. It is not easy to track them. Given where they live, their straight vertical burrows are somewhat deep, getting to a depth of about 2m. Also known as Anecic, this group of worms is normally reddish-brown in colour. They are big and range between 8 and 15cm in length. When they invade a forest, they can have a significant effect of its floor as they have capacity of consuming large quantity of food on regular basis. A typical example of a species of earthworm that belongs to this class is *Lumbricus terrestris* which is normally found around the Great Lakes Region.

With this, I will end my discussion on worms, their anatomy and species here. The discussions in subsequent chapters will dwell more on worm farming.

Chapter 3. Establishing a Farm for Your Worms

To grow and herd worms, you will have to provide them with a suitable farm. A worm farm is not the same as a plant farm. It can be an ordinary container to be kept in an indoor environment or trenches excavated in an outdoor environment or a bin buried on the ground. It is of crucial importance for your worms to feel comfortable and protected from predators and elements of weather in their homes regardless of where it is located or what it is made of. If these conditions are not met, the bin will turn into a graveyard for worms. They will not survive their captivity for a long time and they will give no benefit, agriculturally and economically. Here, I am going to discuss the housing system of worms, its types, factors to consider when choosing one, the best place to locate your worm farm, the winter and summer housing requirements of worms and the general environmental conditions that affect the growth, general health and breeding of worms.

Worm Bins and their Types

As the term suggests, worm bin is any bin or container where worms are grown. In the simplest term, it is a home or a housing system designed for the farming or growing of farms. Worm bins are available in different kinds to suit different requirements. You need to first of all determine a worm housing system that is most suitable for you before you order for your worms. This should not be a herculean task even for newbie. A good number of worm farm and worm dealers sell their worms together with a bin suitable for their survival in captivity.

So, there is nothing to worry about if you will not be able to make a sound decision on this. My first worm bin came with the first herd of worms that I farmed. If you perform a Google search on worm bin, you are going to obtain an impressive result. There are many online stores that sell them. They are also sold in offline worm stores. I am going to tell you the essential features to look out for when you are purchasing your worm bin. But before that, let me describe briefly the various kinds of worm bins.

Types of worm bins
Worm bins differ in their design, style and materials used in creating them. Here are various kinds of worm bins to choose from.

Traditional worm bin
As implicit from the name, this is a kind of container used when worm farming was at the budding stage. These classic designs of worm bins are still available and widely used today, though they are among the oldest types of worm house. It is normally constructed with plastic materials. It does not have to be fancifully designed as worms live in just about any container. You can even transform common household containers such as plastic restaurant tubs, kitty litter containers, plastic buckets and the likes into a worm bin. The essential features that you should include in any container that you would want to use here are a cover to forestall the worms from escaping, vents for proper air circulation, spigots and drainage holes for removal of moisture in order to make harvesting much easier. One advantage of traditional worm bins is that they are inexpensive. Also, creating one is also quite simple as they are simple without any sophistication in design, features and structures.

On the negative side, due to the lack of state-of-the-art features, harvesting worms from this kind of worm bin can be somewhat challenging. Another drawback to this kind of worm bin is that they are normally heavy and water logged.

Bathtub worm farm

This is a fanciful design of worm farm with multiple purposes. It features a bin for the worm which is designed like a bathtub. Beneath it is a storage space where you can put the worm juice-like manure. This worm housing can also be used as a table where gardening jobs can be done or a table for potting up.

Wheelie Bin Worm Farm

Wheelie bin worm farm is another design of worm bin with multiple functionalities. It is suitable for large scale worm farming as it is spacious enough to accommodate thousands of worms at the same time. It also has storage space for food scraps. One good aspect of this kind of wheel bin that gives it an edge over the other kinds of housing system for worm is that it comes with wheels for enhanced portability, flexibility and mobility. Despite its size, one can easily move it about from one location to another. Given this feature, the worm farm is an option for people and businesses that may have a need to be moving their warm farm about. It will also be very suitable for businesses that rent worm bins.

Flow through worm bin systems

The flow through worm bin system is designed to make up for some of the imperfections of the traditional worm bin. It is a good housing system for the farming of earthworms that live on the earth's surface. In this design of worm bin, the worm and organic material or food scraps are placed on top of the bin. But the beauty of the design is that the harvesting of the worm casting is carried out from the bottom. The normal materials used in constructing this type of bin for keeping worms include plastic barrels, wooden boxes and a metal drum.

The bin's bottom is left uncovered with a network of wires, dowels and pipes horizontally running through it just above the opening. To stop the worms as well as the bedding from falling through, the top of the system is covered with a layer of cardboard or paper. The worms are provided nourishment from the top and when they are processed, the manure and casting of the worms are removed from the bottom.

I have a flow through system and love it as it reduces the difficulty involved in harvesting of worms and removal of waste and casting. In fact, many prefer this type of worm bin for this reason. Buy it if you can afford it. It is also not very difficult to be constructed at home. You only required the basic do-it-yourself skills and tools. Check the plan and profile online to see if it is something that you can do by yourself if you are talented in construction.

The Styrofoam Worm House
The Styrofoam worm bin is an option for people on budget. It features layered boxes which are with openings that serve as drainage. The box at the bottom does not have any opening. The mineral-rich worm juice enters there which you will use to manure your garden if you have any.

Stacked bin worm bin systems
A stacked worm bin should be a nice choice for any person with limited space, as it does not take up much floor space. In this type of worm housing system, a number of trays or containers for the worms are vertically stacked on each other. The base that holds the trays serve not just as the foundation but also as a container for collecting moisture. Each of the bins stacked together has a bottom with homes to enable the worms to move from a base to the one on top when bedding and food has been processed and turned into castings.

Worm harvesting in this type of bin is very easy and efficient because the worms move from the bottom bins to the top bin once the waste procession is completed. The top of the structure is lidded and this enhances the moisture retention capacity of the system. There is spigot or drain at the bottom of the system which makes the collection of the worms' juice easy. Liquid is also easily drained out of the system through the spigot at the base of the system. Stackable commercial worm bins are available in different designs with different price tags. If you prefer this type of worm housing system, you should budget between $50.00 and $100.00. If you are skilful in construction, you can build this type of worm farm by yourself. It can be constructed with litter buckets, kitty or wood container.

Outdoor worm bins

If you prefer growing your worms in an outdoor environment, there are also different kinds of outdoor worm housing systems to try out. A typical example of a widely used outdoor worm bin is the above ground design. It is a flow through system or a large bin which has a temperature controlled feature useful in keeping the environment favourable to the survival of the worms throughout the year. There are some that are simply insulated to maintain the right temperature for the worms. In this type of system, the procession of organic waste depends on the naturally generated heat or insulation within the system.

Another example of outdoor worm bin is the in ground system. The entire housing system in this type of bin is buried in the ground. The housing system can be vermitrenches, buried bin or windrows. A buried bin is simply what it sounds like. In this type of system, a bin where the worms will be housed is buried on the ground with its top maintaining level with the ground. In order to ensure that your worms do not escape from their house, you have to ensure that a favourable condition is maintained. Windrows, which are sometimes referred to as vermitrenches, are in the form of long straight holes dung on the ground. Bedding and foods for the worms such as decomposing vegetables and kitchen waste are placed inside the trenches in layers.

After the worms are put inside there, they are covered with more bedding. During the hot period, the trenches should be covered with straw or layer of leaves which will provide the required insulation. The heat of decomposition together with these insulating stuffs will provide the worms with the required warmth and most favourable environment for survival throughout the heat period.

Factors to Take Into Consideration When Choosing a Worm Bin

It can be somewhat challenging for newbies in worm farming to determine which type of worm bin to use. It is important that you use the right bin but choosing one does not have to be a nightmare.

Worms can live in just about any container insofar as the inside condition is suitable for their survival. There are some factors to take into consideration when choosing a worm bin to ensure you get one that will offer your worms the most suitable environment.

The location of the bin

The first important factor to consider before you purchase your bin is where it will be kept. Vermiculture can be carried out in an indoor environment, in a sheltered building with no cooling or heating system or in an outdoor environment. There are bins suitable for each of the environments. In deciding where to keep your worm's bin, you should consider the type of worm farming you want to engage in (is it going to be a large scale worm farming or not) and the available space. For example, if you are planning for large scale worm farming, you should consider an outdoor location or sheltered building. But if you are growing a small number of worms just for the management of your kitchen waste, you may consider an indoor worm bin. A good location should also have the right environmental conditions that favour the survival of worms which will be explained in details later in this chapter.

Don't waste money on stylish and fussy worm bins

As mentioned above, worms can live in any bin insofar as the internal condition favours its survival. They don't care about the look of their bin. By human standard and evaluation, they are messy. That is their nature. Unless you want something that will improve the beauty of your home décor, you don't have to waste money on worm containers simply to get a fancy one. Just look around you to see if you can turn an old container into a housing system for your worms. A container of about 10 litres or 2.64 gallons is what you need to get started.

There is nothing wrong with using a nice looking bin as the housing system for your worms. But it does not make any sense to exceed the limit of your credit lines or to go starving just to purchase a container that you can always improvise from with a container around the house. Note that the wellbeing and health of your worms are not determined by the beauty of the housing system you are using.

The survival of your worm largely depends on the condition and internal temperature of your container. So, spend your money wisely in this regard. Just find a container with the right environment. Its appearance does not matter at all.

Consider the available space
A good container should be roomy for the number of worms housed inside it. Worms don't do well in a congested environment. Ideally, your container should be big enough to accommodate about 1000 worms regardless of the number you are starting out with. Worms reproduce and populate quickly. Even if you start with few numbers of worms, they will increase and multiple within a couple of months. The dimension of a container that can hold such number of worms or even up to 15000 worms is about 49cmL x 35cmW x 20cmH. Being spacious is different from being bulky. I will not advise you to use a bulky or bigger size bin. This is because of the problem of mobility. If you are using a bulkier bin, the worms, bedding and waste produced will make it to be heavier. With its weight, one person may not be able to handle it.

Consider its security features
Security here refers to protection of the worms against a couple of factors. Before you choose a bin, it is necessary that you consider the amount of protection the worms will receive against extreme temperatures, protection against the elements of weather such as sun, heat and floods. Any worm bin that does not provide all these forms of protection to worms is bereft of completeness.

Moisture is important: You should ensure that you purchase a container that has the capacity to keep the environment moist. This is important because without moisture, your worms will dry out and die.

Don't choose or use a transparent container
Some people want to be viewing their worms as they turn their waste into agriculturally important substances. If you want to see your worms, you have to make time to view them from the top opening of their home. Using a transparent container is not good for the survival of most species of worms. This is because a good number of them

are highly sensitive to light. Using a transparent container will lighten up their home, which is not good for them.

Get a container with a lid that fits tightly
Another important feature of a container to consider before choosing it is the lid. A good worm bin should be lidded. If it does not come with any, then you have to provide it with one. The lid should fit properly and tightly. But it should not be airtight. With a lidded container, there is no chance for your worms to escape captivity. Besides, it is a veritable means of preventing loss of moisture through evaporation and other natural means. It also helps to make the container dark, as worms are affected by light.

Don't overlook ventilation
It is important for your worms' home systems to be well aerated and ventilated. Thus, before you choose a container, ensure that it comes with features that will allow for easy air circulation. There should be tiny holes by the side of your containers and at its base. The holes at the base are to drain out the worm tea but they also help in air circulation. There should be about a dozen holes. The holes' size should not be more than 1/6 inches otherwise, they may create an escape route for the worms. So, if you are creating your own bin, it is important that you take this factor into consideration.

The Best Location to Establish A Worm Farm
As I have mentioned above, a worm bin can be kept indoors, in shielded space or outdoors. You don't have to spend money in order to create a suitable location to place your bin. You can keep it in your garden, garage, store room, stoop, cellar and the likes. What is important is to ensure that the location is conducive for their survival. The question that I have to answer here is "what constitutes a conducive environment for the survival of worms." A nice location to keep your worm farm should meet the following requirements.

Protected from extreme temperatures
For your worms to grow and deliver the required yield, they have to be protected from extreme temperatures, that is the summer high heat and winter cold (I will tell you more about the winter and summer home requirements of your worm later). Worms are affected

by extreme temperatures. Thus, a nice location to keep their container is one that offers them protection against high temperature.

Flood free

This is of particular concern to outdoor worm growers. If you are planning on outdoor worm farming, you should ensure that you keep the worms' bin or dig your trenches in an environment that is free from floods. You risk drowning your worms and your entire worm containers flush out if you build a home for them in a location that is prone to floods. Outdoor worm farming is not an option for people living in areas prone to floods unless they will keep their bins in places that are protected against floods.

Free from direct sunlight

I have mentioned above that most species of worms are sensitive to light and are also affected by extreme heat. If the temperature of their environment becomes very high, they are likely to die or suffer greatly. So, you should take exposure to sunlight when deciding on where to keep your worm bins into consideration. Ideally, and as a rule of the thumb, you have to keep your farm bin in a shaded location such as inside a store room, under a roof or a tree and the likes. If your bin is in the garden and you have no tree or any shade there, I will advise you to ensure that the bin is lidded. In this way, you will protect them from the scorching heat of the ultraviolent rays of the sun.

Protection against natural predators

Worms are almost at the lowest level in ecosystem service. A lot of other living things feed on worms. So, a nice location to place their bin is one that protects them against natural predators such as birds, lizards, ants and others. Given the importance of this topic, I dedicated a chapter to conservation of worms where I will tell you more about natural predators to worms and how to protect your worms against them. For now, bear in mind that many animals feed on worms and as a worm grower, it is your duty to protect them against such predators. This cannot be done with pesticides or insecticides otherwise you risk killing your worms. The best means to offer maximum protection to them is to build them a home that protects them from these natural predators.

A Look at worm bedding

Worm bedding is a very important part of a worm housing system. This is why I deem it right to talk it about it separately giving a little detail about it. Worm bedding refers to the first layer of the bin which serves multiple purposes to the worms. First, it serves as a place of refuge for the worms when the upper layers of bin becomes uninhabitable or too acidic for the survival of the worms. This function tells you how important the bedding is in a worm bin. The bedding is also a source of nourishment to the worms. It is normally made from a carbon-base material which will gradually decompose and becomes a source of nourishment to the worms as it contains a certain amount of minerals and protein, but not as much as the feedstock for worms. However, unlike kitchen waste and other nourishment provided to the worms, it takes a longer time for it to break down.

The bedding also helps to maintain air pockets in the housing system of worms. The layer of the bedding is normally consisted of a coarse material which, unlike feedstock, contains mineral and proteins. Thus, it should not be stuffed tightly which does not give room for better air circulation. Another function of the bedding is to absorb excess moisture from the feedstock. Note that your worms will die if the bedding does have the capacity to absorb excess moisture or if it loses this capacity. In order to prevent this from happening, it is of crucial importance that you moisten the bedding material to a level that it will feel like a wet sponge. When such feedstock is place on top of bedding not well dampened, they will produce moisture that will overshadow the bedding's ability to absorb excess water, which will result in the death of your worms.

Suitable Materials to Be Used for Bedding

Not every material can be used as a bedding material. When preparing the bedding of your worm bin, it is of crucial importance that you make use of a good material for such purpose. Here are some of the materials that are a good fit for bedding.

• Shredded black/white newspaper: Many people will tell you that newspapers and cardboard papers are good materials for bedding. Yes, they are good materials but I must emphasize here that not all of them are good materials for bedding. Don't use a paper with lots of colours or any that is glossy. This is because the worms feed on their bedding as well. So, the colour may cause harm to the worms. Black or white coloured newspapers are the best.

• Manure of at least 6 months old: The best type of manure to use is horse manure because it has a low nitrogen content when compared with poultry manure. You can also use rabbit or goat manure but they are not as good as horse manure. Another important feature of horse manure that gives it an edge over other types of animal manual is that it is lighter and better aerated when combined with hay and straw. Horses are given Ivermectin to eliminate intestine worms. This should not frighten you or stop you from using horse manure as your bedding. Many have concerns about Ivermectin affecting their worms. I have used horse manure for many years now and it has not affected my worms in anyway. Besides, there is no study or scientific evidence that suggests the contrary.

Instead, many studies have given indications that Ivermetin is unlikely to affect worms, whether in captive or in the wild. This is because it has been found that the chemical does not take time to degrade when manure becomes exposed to sunlight or hot-compost. The half-life of the chemical in sheep manure is between 7 and 10 days. This is why the chemical does not build up in manure-amended soil. The implication of this is that you should ensure that your manure is aged or up to 6 months old as suggested above. In this way, you will avoid the possibility of your worms being affected in anyway by the chemical.

• Shredded junk mail, cardboard: If you are using cardboard or junk mail, I will advise you to soak it in water before using it. This will help to soften the glue used to bind the layers to make it more breathable. When the bed is made, you should also moisten it with water because of its high protein content derived from the glue.

• Crushed and dried corncobs are also good bedding material.

• You can also use crushed dried leaves. Leaves of some trees such as elm, cottonwood, willow and maple are the best. This is because they can easily be piled up.

- Chopped pea or bean vines

- Black topsoil or loamy soil

- Mixture of sawdust, ordinary soil, peat moss and shredded leaves (they should be moistened).

Materials to Avoid

- Fresh manure from any animal: This is because they can contain some chemicals that have not degraded. Besides, when manure is unexposed to outdoor conditions, it is susceptible to ammonia volatilization. Ammonia can decimate your earthworms. It is a dangerous chemical to most animals, including worms. In fact, due to the problems associated with manure, such as high salt content, I will advise you not to use it at all unless you are an experienced worm grower. If you prefer using it, make sure that you use one that is aged by at least six months.

- Don't use straw. It is not a good bedding material because it has low absorbency capability. Besides, it takes ages to decompose, meaning that it will still be present in the bin when all feedstock have decomposed. You can use that in your poultry nesting boxes.

- Aromatic leaves such as pine, black walnut, sequoia, citrus, laurel, oak, eucalyptus and others should not be used because of their nitrogen and moist content. Some of them are also rich in minerals. However, the major problem with them and why they should not be utilised as bedding material is because they take longer to decompose and they also contain certain substances that are dangerous to worms. Typical examples of such substances are tannic acids, oils and resinous saps. Worms can move away from their beds if they are made from these materials.
- Brewery mash
- Fresh grass
- Coconut coir

Preparing Bedding for Your Worm Beds: Tips

For bedding to serve its purpose, it has to be properly made; not just with the right materials but with the right quantity. If it is not properly prepared, your worms are at risk. This is why it is very important that you get it right. The tips given below will be of help to you.

The lbs of the initial bedding should be about 4-6lbs if the size of your bin is 2'x2' (5.08x5.08cm). For a bin of 2x3inches (5.08x7.62cm), you should set down about 9 to 14 lbs (4.082 to 6.35) of bedding. In other words, the heap of the bedding depends on the size of your bin. As a rule of the thumb, the bedding heap should not be small otherwise it will not be able to absorb the moisture that will be generated by the decomposing feedstock. On the other hand, it should not be too large, else it consumes the space meant for the feedstock which contains more nutrients than the bedding. So, you have to use the right quantity of the right material.

I have already listed the right materials to be used above. There may be other good materials not listed here. Before you use any material, make sure that it meets the right requirement. A good material should not be toxic. It should be absorbent and decomposable. But its decomposition rate should be slower than that of the feedstock. It should be free from chemicals such as ammonia and salt as well as insecticides and pesticides. Other characteristics of good bedding materials are:

- It should have a neutral pH level.
- It should not have abrasive or sharp content (worms have soft and delicate skins which can be punctured by sharp objects)
- A good bedding material should allow air (oxygen) to flow easily through it.
- It should be edible to the worm (in fact, worms obtain a considerable percentage of their nourishment from their bedding).

One important factor that will determine the type of material to be used for your bedding is the species of worms that you are farming. A material may be good for a species of worm but harmful to another species. If you will be growing red worms, manure bedding should be a nice option for you. But take note of what have been said above about how manure should be and the type of manure to use. Suffice it to mention that hot manure, be it horse, rabbit, cow or poultry manure should not be used for red worms. You can also make use of newspapers and cardboard paper, which has to be soaked before being used. Before using the soaked paper, allow the water to drip out. Jersey Jumpers as well as Alabama Jumpers need bedding made from course and dense soil. Mix mulch, top soil and manure together.

Bedding of 4 inches made of dirt and peat is suitable for the African Night Crawler. Apply a lot of lime every week to prevent the bedding from becoming acidic because this species of worms does not like acid. Northern Crawlers need top soil bedding and should be top fed. They are a delicate species of worm and therefore should be handled with caution. They live in tunnels and don't require a heavily moistened environment. So, if you provide them with heavy watering, they will definitely die.

Though each species of worm prefer bedding made of certain materials, they all have similar characteristics and nature and thus each can serve as a substitute for the other. Given this, I will advise you to use a mixture of materials for your bedding in order to establish a balance. This is because some of the characteristics are well pronounced and manifested strongly in some materials than in others. For example, some have a higher absorbent rate while some decompose easily or contain richer nutrients than others. So, if you use a mix of them, they will complement each other.

Now that you know the type of materials to be used as your bedding and how to identify them through their characteristics, the next task is to learn how to use them to prepare suitable bedding. It is not all that difficult to make worm bedding as not much is required. It is as simple as getting the materials you want and mixing them together. Once you obtain a perfect mixture, wet it down. I have mentioned it above and I need to highlight it here again. It is important for your worm bedding to be moistened to avoid the death of your warms. The first reason why the material should be wetted is to enable the worms to get oxygen.

When I was discussing the anatomy of worms, I mentioned that worms do not breathe with their mouth or nose. They get the oxygen they require to live through their body. Their body produces liquid that gets them wet as this is the only means through which they can obtain oxygen. By keeping the bedding damp, you will help their body not to dry out and this ensures that they get a regular supply of oxygen. Another reason why it is important that you keep their bedding damp is to fasten the decomposition of the bedding material and feedstock. If the bedding is not wet, it will take ages for it to be broken down.

Note that wetting down here does not mean saturating them with water or getting them soaked with water. They should be as wet as damp sponges. Just slowly add some water on the bedding using a hand held spray or any other suitable material of similar nature. Collect a few portions with your hand and squeeze it tightly. If you are able to squeeze out a couple of drops of water, stop. The mixture is ok to be used for bedding. If you have added too much water, keep the mixture outside to dry a little. Redo the test as explained to make sure the mixture don't over dry. Lay the bedding on your bin ensuring that the heap is as instructed above. Leave the bedding for about a week to settle and for the temperature to normalise and the acidic level to stabilize. You can now place your worms inside the bin.

Note that this is just one method of preparing the bed. Methods vary depending on experience, the type of worms being farmed and the nature of the container to be used for the ant growing. So, you will also find other ways of making worm beds online. But regardless of the method you are using, the same requirements still stand.

Environmental Conditions that Affect Worms' Wellbeing

The growth of your worms, their general health and reproduction rate depend to a greater extent on certain environmental conditions, which include temperature, moisture, aeration, light and pH level of their housing system. I have and will be mentioning these factors for one reason or the other throughout the course of this book. But because of their importance in worm farming, it will be nice to briefly explain them individually.

Temperature: Worms can survive in an environment with a temperature range of 85 degrees F (29.44 degree C) to 90 degrees Fahrenheit (32.22). However, you can vary this temperature to get a particular result. If you are into commercial worm farming and you will want more cocoon production and hatching, then you should get the temperature of your bin to be between 60 degrees F (15.56 degrees C) to 70 degrees F (21.11 degrees C). For enhanced growth and optimal activity, the temperature should be within the range of 60 to 80 degrees F (15.56-26.67 degrees C). Any temperature range higher or above these ranges mentioned here will affect the health of your worms. Always check the temperature of the housing system of your worms, especially during the summer and winter periods to ensure that they do not fall to any of the extreme levels.

I suggest that you purchase a soil thermometer which is sold at around $7.5 (£5.76) to $8.5 (£6.53) depending on the quality, size and type. Don't use normal body thermometer as the bedding is a different environment from the outside environment and it tends to be cooler.

Aeration: Proper airflow is very important in worm bins because without oxygen, the chances that they will survive are very low. Normally, earthworms can live in oxygenated water or in a condition of low oxygen and high carbon dioxide but never without oxygen. But note that it is not good to keep the bed soaked up as such a condition can result in the depletion of oxygen, a condition that will result in the production of toxic substances by anaerobic bacteria. In general, a nice environment for earthworms should have a lot of oxygen.

PH level: pH in science is a term used to express the acidity and alkalinity of a medium or a substance. Earthworms grow in an environment that is neither too acidic nor too alkaline. You should ensure that that pH level of your bin is within 4.2 to 8.0. If it is below 4.2, then it is acidic and not good for your worm. On the other hand, if it is above 8, it is alkaline. You can balance the acid level by mixing your bedding material with limestone. If you are into commercial production, keep the pH level to 7.0. It is very simple to determine the pH level of your worm bed. Just perform a simple litmus paper test. You can also purchase a pH kit from a feed store. In sum, a good environment that favours the survival of earthworms should be neutral.

Lights: I have mentioned above that worms don't like lights or being exposed to light. You can turn worm abhorrence of light to your benefit. Changes in weather conditions can make the worms try to escape from captivity. This sometimes happens during warm temperatures and high humidity. You can stop them from making such an attempt by just placing lights around the sides of the bin.

Moisture: As already mentioned, earthworms require moisture in order to breathe and move. Thus, they do well in a damp environment. When worms are fully established and you want them to make more cocoons, leave the bed to dry until the top 2 inches are barely damp. Restore moisture in the bed by sprinkling water on it. Note that the body of a worm consists of about 75 percent water.

Thus, the moisture level of your bedding should be up to this level so that the tiny creatures will not find it difficult to breathe, decompose and feed on organic matter. It is difficult for some people, especially beginners, to determine when their bedding has 75 percent moisture. I have already given you a formula to determine the moisture content of the bedding when I discussed bedding and its preparation. Just collect a handful of already prepared bedding and try squeezing water out of it. If you are able to squeeze out a drop of liquid from it, then it is ok. Another more scientific method of determining this is to add 1.5kg (3lbs) of water to every 1kg (2lb) of bedding mixture.

Summer Housing Requirements of Worms

The summer is a period of great heat. Sometimes, the mercury will go very high to the level that will become unfavourable to your worms. But since they are in captivity, they cannot do anything for themselves. It is your duty as their grower to protect them against the scorching heat of the sun by making their home comfortable for them. The best way to go about this is to provide them with shade. There are a number of ways through which you can go about this. Depending on the weather conditions of your locality and the initial location where their home was before, you may consider keeping your worms' bin under a tree to offer the required shade. You can also keep them under a sun roof or a shaded space or in a location that gets little sunlight.

A place that receives a limited time of sunshine, which may be during the morning hours or afternoon, is also ok for that. However, if you cannot find a space like the ones mentioned here, then you have to go for a custom-made sun protection. Here are various ways of providing shade to your worms during the hot winter days.

Using a polystyrene box is a veritable means of protecting your worms from high summer temperatures.

Another inexpensive means of shading your worms during the summer period is to spread second hand carpets on top of their bins as long as the bins are strong. If you cannot find any fairly used carpet, you can achieve the same purpose with wooden boards. A shade cloth normally sold by large garden suppliers and nurseries is also a suitable material that can be used to set a roof over the bin as well. However, this alternative is the most expensive means of protecting your worms from high temperatures. You must not purchase a shade cloth if any of the other alternative means mentioned above is a possibility for you. It does not give you much advantage.

In case the temperature becomes very intense and goes above 35 degrees Celsius (95 degrees Fahrenheit), you need to go the extra mile to offer your worms strong protection against heat because such high temperature is very detrimental to your worms. One of the things to do is to increase the heap of your bedding as a means of insulating the bins against heat. It also provides a large room for the worms to hide deep inside the bed as they look for a more calming environment. In other words, ensure that there is proper air circulation in your bin. There are various ways of increasing airflow in your worm bin. You can keep the bin open. But watch out for predators such as birds, chicken (if you have any), flies and others. Alternatively, you should increase the number of holes in the bin. Install a computer fan in the lid of your worm container. But it is the type of bin that you have that will determine whether or not this approach is suitable for you. It is most suitable for people using a flow through worm composting bin.

Get an electrician to do the basic wiring for you unless you can do that by yourself. You can make it more sophisticated by adding a thermostat to turn the fan on when the temperature rises to a certain level. If installing a fan is not an option because of the bin type you are using, but you still prefer this option, there is no cause for alarm. Just position your bin under a fan or keep it in space with a cooling facility. To use this method, make sure that the moisture level of your bin is up to the required level. More ventilation will result in increase in the rate of evaporation, which implies that more moisture will be lost for the temperature to come down.

When your bin becomes too hot and you need to quickly bring the temperature down, simply throw some ice in there. But this should be done with caution. Ice turns into water when it melts. It means that you are adding more water into your bin. So, don't add too much ice to avoid flooding your bin.
You should also moisten their food and ensure that they remain moistened for a long period of time during the hot weather. You can also increase the moisture level by spraying water inside the bin using a watering can or spray bottle. From your basic knowledge of the science, you know the effect of evaporation. It causes a cooling effect. Thus, as the water evaporates, your worms will feel cool.

Another problem that you will encounter during the summer period is increase in the number of flies and mites that come to your to bin to look for food and a breeding site. Normally, the summer time favours these insects. Thus, they are normally on the increase during the months of summer and they are easily attracted by food scraps smell. Thus, if you are not able checkmate them, they are likely to take over your worm bins and breed in them. I am going to talk about flies in a different chapter. But suffice it to mention that they will constitute a problem to your worms during the summer period and you should brace up for action on how to get rid of these tiny insects.

Earthworms normally breed more during the summer period. So, expect more hatchlings and be ready to welcome the new wriggling herd into the world. One point to bear in mind here is that adult earthworms are not good parents, even though they breed a lot. The baby worms start taking care of themselves from the time they are hatched. To worsen their situation, their parents don't like staying with them. They seem to despise them and thus don't mingle with them. This attitude makes the baby worm move to the top. So, if you don't want to set up a new bin for your new brood, then you have to ensure that they have it all rosy in the bin during the hot period by keeping them cool and comfortable.

The steps to take in order to keep worms safe and secure during the summer can be summarized in these five different phrases, more moisture, more depth, more shade, more protection and more harvesting. If you take these steps and also shade your worm bin, they will remain safe during the hot period of summer. Fortunately, your worms will tell you whether they are feeling alright or not. Though they do not talk but they will begin to act in a manner that will tell you that they are not comfortable with the internal temperature of their bin. When the temperature rises above 80 degrees Fahrenheit (26.67 degrees C), your worms will begin to eat less.

They become less active and reproduction will decrease. If the condition does not improve and the temperature shoots up above 80 degrees Fahrenheit (26.67 degrees C), they will begin to die gradually. There will be mass exodus if they are able to find any escape route. If you notice that your worms are not eating well, it is not a sign that they want a change of food or more food. So, don't increase the quantity of food you give them or your bin will turn into a compost (note the difference between a worm farm and a compost). You know the consequences; you are cooking your worms.

Winter Housing Requirements of Worms

The winter is a period of great cold which affects various animals including worms. In fact, it is a time of the year when a lot of animals in the wild die. Even human beings are at risk. Worms are not exempt. So, if you are keeping worms, it is also very important that you protect them from the terrible cold of the winter season, especially if you are living in a location that is hit by heavy and frequent snow fall. You start offering protection and insulation to your worms once the mercury begins to fall below 5 degrees Celsius / 41 degrees Fahrenheit. If you leave them unprotected under such a condition, they will die. Despite the fact that earthworms can survive extreme temperatures, they are not immune to cold. While in the wild, the earth under which they live protects them.

What to do in order to protect your worms against extreme cold depends on the weather condition of your locality. If you are living in a mild climatic zone which does not experience a temperature of 0° Celsius (32° F), you don't have much to worry about as you have simple task to accomplish for your worms to remain protected. All you have to do is to provide more insulation to your worms by increasing the heap of the bedding inside their bins.

Also add enough food for them, which will also increase the insulation against cold in their bin. The protective barriers provided by the bedding should be up to 12 inches (30.48cm) from all angles. Thus, when the temperature becomes very cold, the worms will move down towards the centre to receive warmth. You can also provide them extra warmth by covering their bins with a blanket or carpet depending on the weather conditions. The worms will still go about their normal business and will be producing eggs and cocoons to populate and perpetuate their kind, unless the temperature drops further down.

However, if you are living in a location where the temperature goes below 5 degrees Celsius (41 degrees Fahrenheit), then you have to do more in order to protect them. First, increase the bedding. With a shallow bed, it is almost impossible for your herd to survive at such a low temperature. Thus, begin on time to get ready for the winter time by gathering the material for more bedding. Besides adding more bedding materials to their bins, there are other things that you can do.

Consider taking the bins inside an insulated room or any indoor facility such as garage, store room and the likes. This ensures that your worms do not freeze to death and that they continue their normal business of decomposing and processing your organic waste during the entire period of the cold months.

If it is not possible for you to move them inside an indoor facility, fill up the entire bin with bedding and food and then cover them with protective blankets or cloth as advised above. While it is good to increase bedding during cold weather as a means of providing more insulation, don't stuff the bed tightly as this will inhibit airflow. Poor ventilation can lead to the death of your worms. Another alternative is to purchase a lidded insulating box made from polystyrene sheets. You can build it by yourself. If you are going to construct one, you should ensure that the thickness of the sheet is about 2 inches to create a better effect.

There are other means to increase the temperature of your bin during the winter period. Offer them more of foods rich in nitrogen because the decomposition of the gas generates heat. You can keep the bin warm with a heat lamp or close to a spotlight. But remember that worms are sensitive to light. So, ensure that their homes are tightly closed if you are using a spotlight. You can also install a warm worm heater. It will be good if you get one that comes with a thermostat so that once the temperature drops to a dangerous point, it will turn on itself.

With any of the above means, you will be able to protect your wiggling friends from freezing. Earthworms exhibit some signs to show that they are feeling uncomfortable during the winter period. When the temperature starts to drop to a level that is very unbearable to them, they will begin to consume less quantity of food. They become less promiscuous and the rate at which hatchling occurs reduces. When their condition worsens, they will go into stasis or torpor which is a state similar to hibernation. I will explain this later. So, during the winter period, begin to watch out for these signs to know if you have got it right or not.

Do worms go into hibernation?

Yes, worms go into hibernation but in a unique manner. Normally, when the temperature becomes unbearable (either too high or too low), worms enter into a survival mode, technically known as estivation. First, they burrow as deep as they can and according to their species abilities, to a point where the condition is more suitable for their survival. They will remain there until the temperature becomes normal. But if the temperature does not improve but deteriorates further, they roll themselves into balls and secrete mucous to cover themselves forming a cocoon like substance that insulates them.

Their bodies' metabolism and functions in such a condition slow down. This is a survival strategy for hot or cold weather. However, they don't remain inside the cocoon forever. When the condition improves, they will break the insulating slime and come out. But if the conditions do not improve or if it becomes worst, after enduring it for a period of time, they will die. So, if you notice that your earthworms have rolled themselves into balls, don't be frightened. They are not dead but they are trying to survive. But it is a sign that if you don't help them to normalize the temperature and if the weather does not improve, they will soon die. Thus, you need to apply the strategy given above depending on whether the situation is caused by extreme cold or heat.

Chapter 4. Getting Your Worms

I believe by now, worm farming is becoming clearer and simpler for you. In the previous chapters, I have examined the pros and cons of vermiculture, differentiated between this practice and other similar practices and examined worm anatomy and three classes of worms. I also explained in detailed the housing requirements of worms both during the winter and summer seasons. It is now time to tell you the best species of worms to farm, the number of worms to start with as a beginner and where to get your worms. I will also teach you how to introduce your worms to their home.

What Is the Best Species of Worms to Farm?

One of the frequently asked questions by newbies in worm farming in various worm forums that I belong to is "what is the best species of worms to farm?". Indeed, contrary to the thinking of many people, special species of earthworms are required for effective vermiculture and vermicomposting. So, you don't just go about digging up earthworms in order to raise them in a bin or to use them to process your kitchen waste. No! It does not work that way, all of them may die. It is therefore important for you to know the right species of earthworms to farm in a worm bin. Some worm species survive in normal garden soil where they feed on soil and organic matters but they will not survive in captivity when kept in a bin.

The most common species of worms to farm in a bin is the Eisenia Fetida. Worms that belong to this species are manure worms, brandling worms, tiger worms, red wigglers and others. Usually, they are available in a variety of colours and sizes. Generally, they are versatile and can survive under different weather conditions starting from a low temperature of 0 degrees Celsius (32F) to a high temperature of 35 degrees Celsius (95F). This, coupled with the fact that they can feed on a variety of organic waste material, makes them easier to manage and good species of worm to start with.

Eisenia hortensis is another species of worm that can be grown in a bin. It is commonly known as the European Nightcrawler. They are bigger in size than Eisenia fetida but exhibit similar behaviours. However, researchers have rated the Belgian Nightcrawlers, as they are also called, lower than the red worms in a number of aspects despite their similarities. First, they don't convert waste into useful products as quickly as the red worms. Their reproduction and growth or maturity rate is also lower when compared with that of red worms. But many growers disagree with this assessment by researchers. They believe that both of them are good. Personally, I cannot give any personal assessment as I have not actually compared them, even though I have farmed both species.

There are other species that you can raise, such as African Nightcrawlers and the Malaysian Blue Worm. But as a rule of the thumb, before you put any species of worm inside a bin for any reason, find out if the species can survive in a shallow system. It is only those species that can do well in shallow systems that you should raise in a bin. Don't try holding any species that are not used to shallow systems in worm bin. If you do, soon or later you will find them dead.

How Many Worms Should I Start with as a Beginner?

As a beginner in worm farming, you don't have to start with a huge number of worms. You have to start with a manageable number to try out your skill and grow your experiences before you can farm huge numbers. However, the number of worms to farm depends on the reason why you want to engage in such a venture. For example, if you want to grow them to manage your kitchen and organic waste, then you have to determine the amount of organic waste that your household generates on a daily basis and also size your trash. It is the amount of waste that you generate that will determine your bin size and the number of worms to put there.

Determining these does not involve any difficult scientific calculation. A square foot ($0.093m^2$) of worm bin surface area will take up a pound (16oz) of kitchen waste. So, if you generate two pounds (32oz) of food wastes for example, two square feet ($0.19m^2$) of the surface area of your worm bin should be able to accommodate the waste. This means that you should get a bin that will accommodate such an amount of waste.

Worms are sold by many stores, not in numbers but in weights. Two pounds (32oz) of worms which are about the weight of 2,000 wigglers are what you need for any pound (16oz) of food waste you produce per day. It is advisable that you start with this number or just one pound (16oz). As mentioned above, worms populate easily. Thus, if you are to provide them with enough nourishment and care, within 3 months, their number is much likely to multiple by twofold.

Note that the quantity to start out as given above is not an exact science. It also, to a certain extent, depends on the species that you want to farm. Another point that I must highlight is that number of worms to put in a bin is determined not by the depth of the bin but the surface area. In other words, a bin with a small depth but with a larger surface area will accommodate more worms than one with small surface area but with a large depth. Another factor that will determine the amount to start with is your purpose of keeping a worm farm. If you are into vermiculture or worm breeding, it is more advantageous to keep a small number of worms in a bin depending on its surface. Provide them with the comfortable environment and enough nourishment as mentioned above.

There will be less competition for food and they will reproduce at a higher rate because they are properly cared for. On the contrary, if you are into vermicomposting, which aims at processing organic matter and production of worm castings, you will require a lot of worms from the beginning. You should also provide a suitable environment. With a favourable environment and lots of worms, it will be easy for a huge quantity of organic waste to be processed and a huge quantity of compost to be produced.

How to Get Your Worms

Worms are not something that you will start looking for in your garden or around your home. Though, they are found almost everywhere, as mentioned above, it is not all worms that are good for farming. Besides, worms look very much alike physically. You cannot rely so much on colour because sometimes, worms of the same species may have different colours. Thus, if you are not a professional, you will not be able to differentiate the various farmable species from other species that cannot be farmed.

Basically, you can obtain your worms through two major ways. First, you can find worms through the Internet. There are a number of web shops that sell worms that can be farmed. There are lots of options and they sell different species of worms such as Night Crawlers, Red Wigglers, Florida Wigglers and even exotic worms. You don't have to worry about the safety of the worms. These web shops ship their worms to their clients using a special type of packaging that preserves them until they are delivered to their owners and transferred to their bin.

However, if you are ordering from the Internet, you should ensure that your worm farm is ready so that once you get your worms, you can transfer them immediately to their bin. But before transferring them, read the seller's instruction on how to open the package and what you should do once you open the package. As it is the case with any other items sold online, you should shop online and find out the options you have as prices and shipping options differ. You should also find out from the seller how long it will take for the worms to be supplied and how long they can stay inside the package.

If you don't want to purchase your worms through the Internet, there is no cause for alarm. There are also offline dealers. They are sold by mainly bait and tackle shops. You can also check and ask people of growers that sell worms within your locality. The easiest means of finding worm farmers within your neighbourhood is to join a worm farmers' forum online. Once you ask your questions, you will get useful answers from the forum members. Also check the phone book listing under worm and worm farmers. You may be lucky to find one close to you.

If you are lucky to find a grower within your neighbourhood, you purchase worms directly from the farm. Buying from a grower directly seems to be the best option because you will receive fresh worms or worms brought out directly from their bin. The grower can also give you some tips on how to transfer the worms to their bin when you get home and other things you have to do to help the worms get used to their new homes. Most growers are happy to share tips with their customers.

Most of the stores that sell worms also sell worm equipment and tools such as worm bins and food. So, in case you will require any equipment or material you can also check for them at the same time from these stores that you are shopping from. You are likely to find a store that sells both worms and equipment. I prefer buying my worms and the equipment that I require from the same shop. Many shops, especially online shops, offer discounts to their customers that purchase a certain number of items from them. Buying them together is a good means of getting a good bargain on your purchase.

Feel free to ask the dealer any questions. Some centres have staff that are specifically employed to provide customers with answers to their questions and clear their confusions.

Introducing Your Worms to their Home

Introducing your worms to their bins does not require any protocol nor should it be a complicated process. All you are required to do is to get your bin ready properly. I have spent time in the preceding chapter discussing how to prepare the bedding. If you are able to prepare the bedding very well, you are good to go. I will not repeat what has been said above. The only point that I have to emphasize here is that you should ensure that you have a proper mixture of the food and bedding material. The right ratio of bedding to food is about 4:3. Note that it is difficult to differentiate food from bedding material because worms also feed on their bedding material.

You can mix the bedding and food in a separate container and when you get your worm bin, you transfer them. You can also mix them directly in your worm bin. After forming the bed and mixing it with food (that is if food and bedding are fresh) leave them for a week or more in order to make it decompose more. As it decomposes, more and more microbes will be produced. The microbes are a good source of nutrients to the worms. During this period, you can be stirring the food occasionally and adding more water if there is a need for that. However, keeping the food to decompose may not be necessary if you are using aged bedding material for the mixture. The microbes are already there. Once the bedding is set, place your worms on top of the bedding. Don't bury them. They will be able to do the rest for themselves. Keep the bin at the right spot with the right environmental conditions as explained above. A new empire is developing in your home to help you manage your waste. Note that at the time when you are preparing the bin or when you have not added the worms, the bin may have a repugnant odour depending on the bedding material. But when the worms start processing and decomposing them, the odour will clear on its own. All you need is to ensure that there is adequate aeration. You should also be mixing the materials periodically for this to happen.

To get the worms to quickly burrow inside the bed when you place them on top, you should leave the bin open and bring it close to a light source. The reason for this should be quite obvious and clear to you if you are reading this book. I have said that worms don't like light. Thus, when you expose them to light, their immediate reaction is to look for where to hide. In this situation, there is no hiding place for them except to burrow inside, which will help them to quickly adapt to the situations they find themselves in. I have used this strategy and it worked perfectly as expected. So, consider it. It will work out for you very well.

If you are using red worms or any other composting species of worm, you shouldn't add much soil to your bedding. Just a pinch of soil to facilitate the growth of the microbes is ok. Adding too much soil will make the bin stuffed, heavy and dense. This will reduce air circulation in the housing system which is not good to the general health of the worms. Besides, using a lot of soil will make the system smell because poor ventilation will turn the system into an anaerobic system, which causes it to become malodorous.

On average, it may take your worms about one to two weeks to settle in their new home. However, bear in mind that situations are not the same. Some expert worm growers can get their worms to settle within the first day of transferring them to their bins. It all depends on how you are able to create a favourable condition for them. Once they find the right environmental conditions suitable for their survival, they will be able to adapt easily and quickly.

Chapter 5. Taking Care of Your Worms

After introducing your worms to the container that will serve as their home, you don't have to leave them to their fate. You need to take care of them, nurture and ensure that they are in the right environment else they will not function optimally and their reproduction rate will be very slow. Worse still, with improper care, they are likely to die while in captivity. In this chapter, I am going to tell you how to take care of your worms, feed them and the various dangers they are likely to be exposed to and what you should do when such issues arise.

How to Keep and Maintain a Your Worm Farm

For your worms to function optimally, apart from feeding them very well, you have to maintain and keep your worm farm in the best conditions. The first thing to do is to ensure that your worms have the best environmental conditions. I have taken time to explain the environmental conditions suitable for the survival of worms. Take a look at these conditions once again and apply all the tips given there. If you are able to keep to the instructions and guidelines provided, your worms will not have any problem with their environment. But maintaining a worm farm is much more than maintaining the environmental conditions. Here are other things you should do.

A good way to manage the moisture level is to have a proper drainage system through which excess liquid is drained out of the bin. Ensure that your bin's tap is open all the time. Keep a bucket underneath it where the liquid will be dripping into. You can also decide to remove the tap completely for water to freely drop into the bucket. Empty the bucket once every week, whether it is filled up or not. If you leave it there, it will develop an offensive odor which will attract flies to your worms' home. Removing it weekly will also forestall the possibility of mosquitoes breeding there. But in case you discover that mosquitoes are breeding there, all you need to do is to pour on top of the water 20 (0.70 fl oz) to 50ml (1.7 fl oz) of your vegetable cooking oil each time you place the bucket under the tap to refill.

Keep the bin lidded. Though, it is not advisable to airtight close the container, it should be properly closed so that the worms will not escape. I normally place a heavy object like a brick on top of the cover so that the worms will not bring it down. You may be wondering how possible it is for worms to be able to raise the cover of their bin and escape. It is a simple task for them to achieve with concerted effort. When they crawl on the lid in a large number, their weight will pull the cover. But if you place a heavy object on the cover, they will not be able to pull it out.

Remove the worm juice once every week. Extracting the juice should be an easy process. Just pour water from the top opening of the worm farm for it to run out from the drainage system. When the juice comes out, don't forget to redo the moisture level test. If the bedding has too much moisture, add more materials to reduce the moisture. Too much moisture can affect your worms in a number of ways. Certain physical changes that occur in worms are indicative of too much moisture in the bedding. They will turn pale in colour. Secondly, they will begin to emaciate instead of looking fat, healthy and nice. There is nothing more to do than to put more bedding materials to absorb the excess moisture.

On the other hand, insufficient moisture content will affect the worm also, as I have mentioned above. Apart from affecting their health negatively, it will also affect the production of worm tea. If you notice that your worm is not producing any tea, you have to bring their moisture level to a balance. With a proper moistened environment, worms are supposed to produce their nutrient-rich juice. What you should do in this situation is to include more bedding material with a higher water content. If your bedding depth is already sufficient, there is no need to add more material. Just dampen them more by springing some quantity of water on them. But be careful not to get the bedding wetted or soaked.

Don't use thick paper to cover the bedding. Instead, it is the best practice to use tumbleweed worm blankets. This is because with thick paper, air circulation will be inhabited. This will affect the growth of your worm. When you want to pour water in the bin in order to extract the juice, you have to remove the blanket first.

You should try to clean the bucket kept under the bin for collection of excess water from the bin. You can do this once every month. In this way, it will not develop bacteria and become infectious to your environment. Another thing you should always do in order to maintain a high level of hygiene for your worms is to remove their castings occasionally. Once you are providing your worms with enough nourishment, they will be producing castings for you. Just like human beings defecate unwanted and undigested food substances from the body, worms also excrete and defecate. Their casting is their faeces.

As worms feast on the kitchen wastes provided to them, they produce castings for you which you can use as manure for your garden. What will tell you when to remove your casting is the bedding of your worms. The bedding provides nourishment to the worms. So, when its level has gone down or when the worms have devoured it, the bin will be left with their casting only. This is the time to harvest it. Normally, this will be between 3 and 5 months. It is important to remove the casting which is known in vermicomposting as the compost. High concentration of the castings makes the environment unfavourable to them. I will explain in detail how to harvest the casting in the last chapter of this book.

Use a trowel to turn over the top layer of your bedding at least once a week or every 10 days. If you are composting in an outdoor environment or in your in garden, then you have to use a shovel. You should be careful while doing this. You don't have to dig very deep when turning the top soil. This practice helps to prevent waste product of worm farming or vermicomposting from getting stuffed and compressed. If this happens, it will inhibit air circulation creating room and a favourable environment for anaerobic bacteria to develop.

There is the tendency for some people to think that worms are messy and therefore no need to keep their bins clean. This is far from the truth. You should occasionally clean their bins. Thus, get a new bin or bins depending on the number you have now. Prepare and set up bedding for them as instructed above and then transfer your worms to these new bins after they have been in the old ones for six to nine months. Clean the old bins properly. Set up new bedding on them and move the worms back there after they have lived for six or nine months in the new bins. But if you don't have more bins and you have no money to purchase new ones, there is no cause for alarm. Just put the worms in a holding container. Clean your bins and move them back. The worms shouldn't stay for more than 3 to 4 days in the holding container otherwise they are likely to die. These containers are for temporary storage. So, if you are going to use the same bins, make sure that you have your bedding materials ready and that they are aged so that you can transfer them back as soon as the bedding is prepared.

Protect your worms from predators, especially insects that will feed on worms. Birds are not likely to attack them since the bins are kept in the homes or shaded place around the home. I am going to talk about worms' predators in another chapter. But for now, it is of vital importance that you keep them safe and secure from these predators. Another crucial point that I should mention here is that the presence of unwanted guests in your worm bin is an indication that something has gone awry. It is important that you find out what has gone wrong. For example, a bed with high level of acidity will attract white flies, fruit flies, white worms and spider mites. This is because these unwanted guests survive more in acidic environments.

So, when you begin to see these unwanted pests, you have to frustrate them by making the environment unsuitable for their survival. Place more fibrous material to balance the acid level. A worm bin that loses moisture can become too dry and such a condition will ordinarily attract ants in the bin. You can chase ants away from your bin by ensuring that the bed is sufficiently moistened. Note there are some guests that are useful to the worms such as maggots and slaters. So, don't drive them out unnecessarily unless their presence has become annoying.

Keep the population of your worms under check. Whether you're farming worms just to manage your kitchen waste or you are doing it for financial benefits, you need to control the population of a worm in a bin. Every bin has a capacity or the number of worms it can accommodate. So, ensure that your bin is not over populated. You don't have to do extra ordinary things in order to reduce the population of your worms. Just follow simple biology. All you have to do is to reduce the quantity of food you provide them with. They will struggle and compete for the available foods. The competition for food will help to reduce the nutrients they obtain and their activities including production among the worms. When you want to increase their population, give them more food. Competition will disappear and they will get more nutrients and make more eggs and cocoons. If you are not planning on establishing a new worm farm, it is advisable that you keep to the number of worms you start with or you allow minimal increase using the tips give here.

Feeding Your Worms

Every living thing feeds and maintains a very good health when there is proper nutrition. The same thing is applicable to worms. It is not enough to provide them with a suitable environment. You should also feed them very well. If they are malnourished, they will not perform optimally and their growth and reproduction will be affected. In other words, proper nutrition is an inevitable part of worm farming that should be taken seriously for optimal performance, high rate of reproduction and good quantity of casting. Let me begin by telling you what to and what not to provide your worms with.

What to and what not to add to your worm bins as food

In feeding worms, quantity and quality matters. Don't just stuff their beds with food and don't just give them any organic waste or any kitchen waste. Below is a list of what to put in their bedding as food and a list of what should be sparingly provided and what should not be provided at all regardless of the circumstance.

What to give your worms as food

- Fruit and veggie scraps
- Egg shells which are rich in calcium are required by worms in order to stay healthy
- Coffee grounds and filters
- Oats
- Corn flakes
- Corn meal
- Corn cereal/bran
- Pizza crust
- Rye meal

- Bread and cheese
- Coffee grounds and tea bags (don't put teabags made from plastic mesh, only paper teabags are good for worms)
- Cooked vegetables, grains, rice, pasta (basically, all vegetarian foods are good but not meat based sauces)
- Newspaper and unprinted cardboard (check the section of bedding to know how they should be prepared) .

Note that certain acceptable worms' feedstock should not be provided in a large quantity.

What not to include in your worm farm
- Fish and meat (this is because they will decay and develop odor which will attract pests such as rats. If you want to compost meat, then you should consider using a Bokashi bin)
- Glossy, bleached or coloured newspaper (the colours and their other chemical contents are not good for your worms' health)
- Fresh manure (for the reasons given above under bedding as a subheading)
- Human faeces
- Oily foods
- Kitty litter
- Bones
- Large amounts of pasta
- Corn cobs
- Large pieces of bread
- Cotton gin waste, except organically grown and processed cotton gin waste

Things to provide with caution
- Pet waste (you can only use this in a worm farm dedicated to decomposing pet dung as they may contain pest)
- Citrus and onions (this should be provided sparingly or not at all)
- Dust obtain from a vacuum cleaner (you can use dust vacuumed from a carpets made from natural fibre material and not those obtained from carpets made from synthetic materials)
- Processed foods (you can only provide it if you are sure that the chemicals used in processing them will not have any effect on your worms).

Tips for Feeding Your Worms

Providing nourishment is simple but somewhat delicate and complex as there are a number of dos and don'ts. It is not a matter of making the bedding and mixing them with some organic matter. Take note of the following important points about your worms' feeding.

Always provide your worms with a quantity of grains that they can consume within a 24 hour period. This is because grains easily sour. When they sour, the acidic level of the bedding will increase and this will make it unfavourable for your worms. They can die depending on their acidic level. If some grains are not consumed after 24 hours, you have to remove and clean the leftover before the next meal. But having leftovers implies that you should reduce the quantity of grains that you give them.

Provide conditions that induce or facilitate the growth of microbes in the bedding as they help worms to digest their food. This is why I recommend the use of horse manure as bedding because horses digest their foods using microbes. Using it as your bedding is therefore a veritable means of having some microorganisms in your worms' bedding. But you can also purchase certain types of liquid soil balancer produced with earthworm casting to increase the microbe level in your bedding. It is quite easy to use. Just spray it over the food. This liquid also helps to eliminate pests like mites and certain worm related concerns such as sour bedding. There are many products you will find in worm stores but I use Vermaplex®.

You should provide your worms with regular nourishment. As already mentioned, worms are heavy eaters. They consume up to 50% of their body weight. But this does not mean that you should over feed them. Adding too much food in the bin has terrible consequences on them as I already mentioned. It will turn the bin into compost which will make the environment unfavourable for the worms. Besides, if you put too much food in their bins, there will be a lot of unprocessed foods there. To avoid having unfinished food, you have as much bins and worms as commensurate to the amount of waste that you generate in your home. So, your worms are processing all your waste, you don't have to force them into doing so by providing them more than what they can consume. All you have to do is to create more worm bins.

Certain food sources such as tomatoes, kiwifruit and others have high acidic levels. Such food sources can be added to their meal but ensure that you balance their acidic levels. You only need to mix them with certain food sources such as egg shells, leaves, agricultural lime granules, fibrous materials such as shredded paper or cardboard, wood ash, sawdust and the likes.

Bury foods at one corner of the bin. Don't just spread the food at the entire surface of the bin. Though this will not constitute any problem if your worms like the food, it is always good to have a space free from food. Worms also make choices. So, if you cover their entire bin with foods they don't like, they will not have any place to stay until the food is removed. This is why it is advisable to keep the food just at one side. But alternate to the side you put food. I said bury the food in the bedding. The reason for this is to prevent the bin from developing odors. As I will explain later, it also helps to prevent flies and certain predators from invading the bin. Besides, compost worms spend much of their time inside their bedding devouring the food. They only come to the surface occasionally.

You may use a trowel to bury the food. But if you are using a trowel, you should be very careful to avoid cutting your worms. The best way to do it is to use your hands. Just get reusable latex gloves. One for one hand is ok but if you like you can get a pair for both hands. In this way, you will prevent dirt and bacteria from getting under your fingernails or getting into your body through wounds and pores on the skin.

Slice and cut the food into smaller pieces rather than leaving them in large chunks. When feeding your worms, you should consider them as babies without teeth. Though they will still consume the food if your leave them unbroken, when they are pieced, there will be more surface area for bacteria to work on the food and break it down.

It is also good to freeze and thaw food before feeding it to your worms. This is because when they are frozen and melted, they become pasty which will facilitate decomposition as it will be easy for the worms to feast on. Note that worms don't have any teeth to bite food. So, if you provide them with fresh food, they will still wait for it to become mushy before they can start to feed on it.

When to feed your worms

One of the major concerns of beginners in worm farming is to know when to feed their worms or how often to feed them. Worms have good appetite and can consume about 50 percent of their weight on daily basis. With this hint, you can calculate how much food to provide them on daily basis. So, if you have a pound of worms, you will need ½ pound (8.oz) of food for them on daily basis. With a pound (16.oz) of food, you can feed 2 pounds (32oz) of worms on daily basis. Multiply the number by 7 in order to get the amount of food that you require to feed them on weekly basis. You can divide this amount into two and feed them twice a week. There are also some people that feed their worms once a week or three times a week. However, as a rule of thumb, before you add more food, ensure that they have finished what was provided to them previously. If your worm farm is in an outdoor environment, you may feed them once in two or three weeks.

I will suggest that you start with a small amount of food depending on the number of worms you have in your bins. Check the food stash in their bedding every other day to see if they have devoured it. Add more to it as they eat. If you don't have enough kitchen waste for your worms, then you have to purchase them. Possible places to look for such foods include restaurants, companies with cafeterias, school and universitie cafeterias and similar places. You can even get them free from some of these places. But ensure that you are getting the right type of foods to feed your worms with. On the contrary, if you have too much food waste to feed your worms, you can freeze them in a freezer bag and use them as need arises.

Remember to avoid over feeding your worms. Worms don't care about their figure but when they have enough they will stop feeding. What is not eaten will rot and this will attract fruit flies.

I am going for a holiday, do I have to put plenty of food in my worms' bin?

The holiday period is always a nightmare to pet owners especially when they want to go to a location that they don't want to travel to with their pets. This is why many beginners in worm farming worry about the wellbeing of their worms during this period. You don't have to hire a worm sitter or over stuff your bin with plenty of food that will last throughout the period of your holiday. Even if you are going to stay away for three weeks or up to a month on holiday, nothing will happen to your worms. Just provide them with their normal weekly nourishment and travel. But before leaving ensure that their bins are in the best of condition and protected. It is only the changes in environmental conditions that you have to worry about.

So, make sure that the climatic conditions will be stable overtime. The meteorology department of your locality can provide you with helpful information on this. Also check other aspects of environmental conditions treated above. But don't worry about your worms dying of starvation unless you are going to stay for months. Once they finish their food, they will start to consume their bedding. Before they will finish it, your holiday will probably be over.

How to Take Care of Worms in Winter

I have exhaustively dealt with housing requirements of worms during the winter. Now, I am going to tell you other things that you need to do during the winter in order to ensure that your worms perform optimally during this period. Here are some useful tips to apply.

Just like humans will always feel the pinch of cold weather during the winter season, worms also feel the discomfort of cold weather. So, when the temperature begins to drop below 60 degrees F (15.56 degrees C), they will become less active and eat less. This is not a time to put enough food for them on the table. Ideally, it is advisable that you reduce the quantity of food that you provide them. This is because, if you provide them with excess food, there will be a lot of leftovers. First, this will give you the added task of clearing unconsumed foods. Secondly, the leftovers can get down and permeate into the bed, increasing its acidity, which spells doom for the worms. Besides, they rot, become malodorous and then attract mites and other pests. Thus, whether you are into worm breeding for sale or into vermicompost, as a rule of the thumb, you should not over feed your worms during the winter. Before you add any food, ensure that the previous ones have been consumed within a space of 1 to 2 days. Don't add any more food unless the previous ones have been consumed completely.

There is the tendency to deny the worms of sufficient oxygen in the attempt to keep them warm during the winter period. So, if you take your worms' bin inside your home or any shaded place, ensure that their housing system is also ventilated. They need plenty of fresh air despite the cold weather.

Don't allow your bedding to get to freezing point before taking the bin inside or to a warm location. You have to send them to a warmer location as soon as the temperature begins to drop.

Check on your worms regularly to know whether they have estivated. As explained above, it is survival mechanism. If they have formed themselves into balls, you are not getting it right. Seek for a professional advice or help if you have nothing to offer them.

When worms are not feeling comfortable, they plan their escape from captivity. Is this surprising to you? Yes, they put energy together in order to lift the lid of their bin. So when you see them grouping together and forming themselves into ball together, they are planning to escape from captivity even though they don't realize that such escape will result in their death. This is why it is important that you check on them on a daily basis during the winter period. You can forestall the occurrence of this ugly situation by providing them with adequate warmth. Ensure that the temperature within their bin does not fall below 40 degrees F (4.44 degrees C).

Note that the winter season is always a trying time for worm growers and people into vermicompost. It is a time that you need to be more watchful and do more to protect your worms from the cold. It requires patience and diligence. With a high sense of duty and dedication, you will be able to help your worms go through the difficult time and safely enter into spring, which offers them the best weather condition.

Caring for Worms during the Summer Period: Tips

The summer season brings its challenges and problems to worm growers. It can be a challenging period for beginners in worm farming as worms can die if things get awry inside the bin. However, if you are able to manage the season very well your worms will go about their normal activities and keep devouring your waste. Note that the summer season does not constitute any problem to some growers. It all depends on your location. You will only have to worry about the season if your location normally experiences high temperatures. The good news about the summer season is that it is the time that the worms produce plenty of cocoons. But they can only do that if they are well taken care of and if you are able to handle all the potential problems associated with the period. Below are certain routines that you should abide by during the summer period, especially when the temperature increases to a level that is dangerous to worms.

Unlike in winter, you should add more food for your worms during the summer season. This is because they are more active during this period and thus they consume a lot of food and produce more hatchlings. Besides, the new members of the colony also need plenty of food in order to grow rapidly into adulthood. As mentioned above, worms are not good parents. So, the adult worms move away from their babies. There is the possibility of the new worms making an attempt to leave the bin. So, you should ensure that they do not escape.

Be mindful of the possibility of a population explosion and the possibility of the bin getting overcrowded. If a bin has more worms that it should, you may consider selling some or starting a new worm farm with some of the worms from the overcrowded bins.

Make the bedding wetter than it was during the winter period. This is because during the summer period, moisture evaporates at a higher rate. This causes a cooling effect. With insufficient moisture, the bedding will become too hot and this can affect the performance of your worms. However, moistening the bedding more does not mean getting it soaked. It simply means that the bedding should always pass the moisture test explained above.

Be on the lookout for the pests associated with the warm period. Hot and wetter weather favours the growth of certain living organisms such as mould and other fungi. At this point, I have to emphasize that moistening up a bed properly or as expected will not provide a favourable environment for these microorganisms to grow. They can only grow if the moisture level is not properly balanced. This is why worm farming should be seen as an art as well as a science. Do it right and you will get the right result. The reverse will also be the case if you don't do it right. Mites are another pest that is commonly seen in worm bins during the summer period. This pest loves acid and thus if your bedding becomes acidic, it is an invitation to these tiny organisms which they will surely honour. Ants are also common during the summer season. But if you can keep the environment clean and properly damp the bedding, they will definitely keep away from your worms.

The only way to protect your worms from any summer related problems is to be watchful and monitor them very well.

Worm Farm Concerns and What to Do

I have dealt with a number of issues in the preceding chapters and in some of the chapters, I have pointed out some of the concerns or complaints beginners in worm farming experienced sometimes and provided solutions to them. Here, I am concentrating fully on the various worm farm concerns.

Rain

This is a problem for people that normally keep their worm bins in an open place. During rainy season, it will shower them. Rain water will enter bins that are not properly lidded. This can give some advantages, as it will help in the extraction of the leachate or worm wee from the bin. However, the problem with this is that it increases the possibility of the bed getting soaked with water. The tips given above on how to reduce moisture also apply here. You should also leave the tap of the bin open. In this way, you will protect your worms from drowning.

Unfavourable temperature

Check the subheading on winter and summer housing requirements in chapter three. They contain useful information on this concern and what to do when they arise.

Insects and ant problems

It is not totally a problem to have certain insects in your worm bin. In fact, some of them have a symbiotic relationship with the worms and thus their presence in the bins is encouraged. Some of these beneficial insects feed on rotten organic matter. They are decomposers as well. Thus, if you are farming worms to produce compost, they are welcome guests. Typical examples of such insects are millipedes, soldier fly larvae, red mites, fishworms and others. However, there are some insects and ants that should not be seen in your bin, as they can attack your worms. The best way to discourage some of these unwanted guests, especially ants, from coming into your worm bin is to ensure that the bedding is damp or sufficiently moistened. This is because these tiny creatures don't like a wet environment. But some ants are resilient and will also find their way through. So, you need to go the extra mile by creating a barrier known as an ant moat.

Depending on the design of your worm bins, you can place them on top of trays of water (if they have legs). The water will prevent them from climbing up. If your bins do not have any legs, you can also use a watering can to spray water around your bin to dampen the corners where it is placed. Insects and ants will feel unsafe in such environments and will not come close. Apply some Vaseline or any suitable gummy substance around the legs of the bin to deter them from climbing up the table leg. You can also apply pyrethrum dust around the bed when there are ants in your bin. Check around the bin to ensure that there is no food spilled closed to the beds. Ants can sense food from afar. Once there are spills, they will be attracted and from the crumbs on the ground, they will go into the bin.

For mites, you only have to make the condition unfavourable for them. They survive more in acidic environments. So, keep to the advised pH level. Mites also like a soaked environment. You know already what to do in this regard to frustrate them out of your worm bins. Additionally, you should avoid including fleshy and wet garbage into your worm bins. It is also advisable that you maintain a feeding routine. Having a bin with a good drainage system is also a must. If there is a build-up of mites already in your bin, remove the cover of the bed and bring the bin under sunlight for a couple of hours. Mix the bed with calcium carbonate once in three days.

Some expert growers also try to get rid of mites and other insects physically or with chemicals. Physically, water the bed to the extent that the pests are flushed out. Pouring excess water inside the bin can also bring up the mites to the surface. Once they are up to the surface, they will be collected and burnt. This method will definitely give some positive results. But I will advise you not to apply it unless you are proficient with it. Similarly, using chemicals to get rid of unwanted insects like mites by force should not be used by a beginner. If you must use such a method, you should ensure that the chemical to be used does not have any effect on the worms.

Odor and smell

I have talked about odor, causes and what to do to prevent it. There is no need to repeat what has been said. So, if you keep to what has been said about that, your bin will not develop any odor or smell.

Fruit flies and other kinds of flies

Flies are also regular unwanted visitors in bins that are not properly managed. Given how quick they can appear and develop in bins, some newbies erroneously think it is impossible to control flies in and around the bin. Don't have such mind-set as it is 100% possible to prevent flies from taking over your bins. First, abide by the tips given here on how to prepare the bed and feed worms. If you do, their chances of developing inside your bin are minimal. In addition, you should try using paper (the type suggested above) to wrap foods for your worms before putting it in your bin. Cover the bin and keep the bin surroundings clean. If the issue continues, you may consider using a natural predator of flies. Spiders are nature predators of flies. So, keep your bin where there is a spider web. But always cover your bins so that spiders will not enter inside it. If they do, you may be treating them to a delicious and free meal.

Black soldier fly/maggots

Some growers consider the black soldier flies and maggots as pests. Maggots are normally seen in outdoor worm farms. This is because soldier fly larvae develop quickly in such bins. However, these larvae are not harmful to worms. They only share their food. But this is a symbiotic relationship because the maggots secrete chemicals that keep flies away from the bins. When they develop into adults the soldier flies are of no consequences as they do not sting and do not eat worms. Besides, their lifespan is very short. An adult black soldier fly lives only about a week. So, if you see them in your bin, you don't have to panic. You may allow them to survive. But if you don't like their presence, you can eliminate them from your worm

63

farm. You only have to make certain adjustments to kill the maggots so that new adults are not formed. Just make the top of your bin dry. Uncover your bins and keep them outside for a while. You can also add more bedding material to soak up the moisture. Once the top is dry, the environment will be unfavourable for them and they will die. If you want to feed your worms during this period, ensure that you bury their food deep inside the bedding. Trap adults and mature flies inside the bin using fly strips.

Moisture can't drain through the tap

I have come across complaints of water tap blockage or moisture no longer draining through the tap in some forums. Sometimes, the tap can get blocked by debris and the worm juice will no longer be dripping out. It is not a big problem. It is something that you can easily resolve. You may consider replacing the tap if you can afford a new one. But if you cannot afford one, just remove the tap completely and leave an opening so that the liquid will freely drip into the collection bucket. Once you have removed the tap, spray water on the bedding to flush out the leachate accumulated throughout the time the tap was not functioning in to the bucket.

Worms processes food wastage very slowly

It may happen that your worms are processing food very slowly when every condition, including the temperature and moisture level, is in order. You can improve the digestive system of worms by spraying a handful of soil on top of the food you will serve them. Worms have a gizzard like birds. With the soil added to their food, they will get more grit in their gizzard and this will quicken the digestion of food. It will also be good if you mix their food with dolomust or worm farm compost conditioner once every week.

Overfeeding problem

Sometimes, beginners make the mistake of over feeding their worms. If you make such a mistake and you notice it, the first thing you should do is to stop feeding them for a while or reduce the quantity of food that you give them. You can help them to digest what they have consumed quickly by spraying a handful of worm farm and compost conditioner product or dolomite on their foods. I personally use dolomust but there are other products. Use a trowel to turn the food. After turning it, spray a few more garden soils on top of it and cover it with worm blanket. This will help to make the processing rate quicker.

The home tray and bottom of the feeding tray having a gap
If you have this problem, just bring out the feeding tray and put more soil on to the surface of the home tray. Instead of soil, you can use potting mix or mature compost. Put back the feeding tray when you have added more soil.

Dead worms
Sometimes, you may open your worm bin and discover that some of your worms are dead and those that are still alive are seriously seeking for an escape route. It is a sign that something is going awry. There is something that you are not getting right. Worms look fragile but they can survive through uncomfortable situations. They also can easily adapt to life in captivity. The only reason why they should die prematurely is because the bin environment is not good for their survival. It may be that the temperature is too high or too low. Poor air circulation and high acid levels can bring about their death. Putting the wrong feedstock in their bedding can also result in their death. The solution to this problem is to find the actual cause of their death. Check the temperature to see whether it is too high or low. Test the moisture level as explained above and do what's needed if it is too high or too low.

A simple litmus paper test will tell you if the pH level is below or above the given range. I have explained above what you should do in either of the situations. Also make sure that they are provided with the right food and in proper quantities. Finding out what has gone wrong may be time consuming, burdensome and daunting. Unfortunately, that is the only thing to do. Some newbies make the mistake of procuring new worms. Replacing the dead ones is not the solution to the problem. If you purchase new ones, they will still die insofar as their living condition is not comfortable for them. Once you are able to create a suitable environment for their survival, the remaining ones will start feeling comfortable and stop making attempts to escape.

Note that it can be challenging, especially for beginners in worm farming, to get everything right and to avoid some of these concerns.

So, if you experience them, it is normal. You don't need to be discouraged about it. Forge ahead and abide by all that has been said here. Gradually, you will begin to get a positive result as you master the act of worm farming.

How to Know that Your Worms Are Healthy and Happy

Worms don't talk and so cannot tell you whether or not they are not feeling fine. But you can tell how healthy they are or how they are feeling from their behaviour. They will display certain signs that will let you know of their conditions. Here are simple signs that your worms are doing great.

Little or insignificant odor: I have read a lot of posts on different forums in which some growers mentioned that their bins are odourless. But based on my experience, it is almost impossible to have a worm bin that is completely without any odor. Normally, well managed worm farms will have a little earthy odor. However, the smell should not be repugnant. You should be able to stay and converse with somebody freely where your bins are. If your bin has a repugnant odor with a lot of flies, then all is not fine. Your worms are not in the best conditions. A worm farm that is in the best condition produces little or no inoffensive odour.

High rate of reproduction: Worms are hermaphrodites in nature and they have good disposition for mating. So, there is nothing that will stop your worms from producing cocoons that will hatch into baby worms except poor conditions and nutrition. Under normal circumstances, your worm will be able to double their population within three to six months, depending on their species. So, if you are not getting new worms in your bins, it is an indication that your worms are not ok. You need to do something to improve their conditions. A worm farm is healthy if it is producing cocoons at a very good rate. Exception to this is when the reproduction is intentionally controlled as instructed above.

Good quantity of compost/castings: you are growing worms to manage your organic waste or just to breed them, your worm farm should be producing a good quantity of organic waste, which includes the worm tea. The rate at which they produce casting and their rich juice shows how well they are fed. As already mentioned

66

above, worms do no other thing in their bin than devour organic waste and process them into compost or castings. So, when they are not giving you as much casting as they should, it may be a sign that they are not well fed.

In summary, worm farms do not require much maintenance. However, this does not mean that you should just keep them in the bins and abandon them there to their fate. You need to also be checking on them to ensure that everything is ok with them. When you notice any of the above signs or you are not getting the required results from them, it is a clear indication that they are not feeling good. With the tips provided here, you will be able to improve their conditions and make them deliver the expected result for you.

What to Do In Order to Grow Your Worms Population

Any worm grower that would want to make money from the sale of worms will definitely want their worms to increase in population at a rapid speed. But this desire is not always realized due to one issue or the other. It will be of grave concern to you if your worms are not making cocoons which will turn into babies. This is because your business will not give you any profit. But since worms normally hide inside their beds, how do know when your worms are making babies as they should and when they are not making any babies? You don't have to bring your worms out from their bins in order to count them to know whether they have increased in number or not. The worms will tell you that through their behaviours. Here are the indices to look for.

Worms are "promiscuous." They mate at random. So, when you don't see them mating as described above, it is an indication that they are not producing cocoons as they can only produce cocoons when they mate.

There are no cocoons in the bins. Worms' egg capsules, which house the growing babies, are very tiny. They are similar to rice in shape. So, check your bin to see if there are cocoons. Worms make eggs throughout the year but their egg making season is during warm weather. So, if you don't see any cocoons, especially during the hot period, your worms are not producing eggs. Something is not ok with the herd of worms in your bin.

Look for the babies themselves. The eggs hatch into baby earthworms, which are smaller in size than the adults. They don't stay with their parents. From birth, they start taking care of themselves. In fact, they are seen alone because their parents don't like associating with them. So, look around to see if you can find small youngsters moving about. However, you should be careful not to confuse malnourished and sick adults with these youngsters. If you cannot find them, then your worms are not procreating as they should.

Your worms should be able to double their size within 3 to 6 months, depending on their species. So, if this is not the case, you have to do something to increase their rate of production. There is nothing more to do except what has been said above on the proper care of worms. If you give your worms proper care and ensure that their environmental conditions are ok, there is no reason why they should not make babies for you. You should also abide by the rules on feeding given above. Also make your worms happy and don't stress or disturb them. Worms that are stressed or disturbed don't do well. For example, keep your worms where they will not be disturbed by noise. If they are not happy, they will not mate and therefore will not produce any cocoons.

Note that worms when in captivity don't procreate and make babies throughout their lifespan. They regulate themselves according to the available space in their home. If a bin is stuffed with worms, they will stop procreating to reduce competition for food and to ensure that available food gets to all. So, it is also good that you divide your worms when they increase so that they will keep procreating. You can sell the worms or use them to start another bin.

Chapter 6. Children and Worm Farming

Can children be allowed to manage worm farms? Is it good for schools to have worm farms? Can managing a worm farm have any effect on children? These and some other questions are not frequently asked by parents who have worm farms in their homes. In this chapter, I am going to look into worm farming in children's world. In the ensuing discussions, some of these concerns are raised and thoroughly ironed out.

Worm Farms in the School: Any Benefits

In many places, schools are encouraged to establish worm farms and composts in the school's premises. There are even some localities that fund the establishment of such farms. Some people cannot understand why schools should go into worm farming, as they don't see them deriving any benefit from such an enterprise. For some people, vermicomposting is something most suitable for farmers and thus schools have no business with it. If you belong to the class of people with such a mind-set, the question that you should answer is "does school produce organic waste? Indubitably, schools produce a huge quantity of organic waste. Thus, it is not a bad idea for schools to have it within their premises to help them manage their waste. The truth is that worm farming gives a lot of benefits to schools. Here are the various reasons why schools should engage in it.

Easy and affordable means of managing waste

Schools generate a huge amount of organic waste on a daily basis or during school hours. Pupils and students come to school with their lunch bags stuffed by parents with different kinds of edibles. They also spend a lot of money in the school cafeteria on snacks. But many children don't consume half of the contents of their lunch. This is common in kindergartens and elementary schools. School cafeterias and dining halls are normally littered with food scraps, which are swept and dumped in the dust bin together with leftovers. Parents are happy to see their children return home with empty food flasks. But the truth remains that a large quantity of this food goes into the bin. Schools without worm farms will have to pay for the evacuation of this waste into the landfill. But they can save a lot of money if they are able to establish their own worm farm where this waste is processed.

Manure for school flowers and garden
As you already know, worm farms produce leachate (worm tea) which is highly rich in plant nutrients. The organic wastes are processed and turned into manure. Rather than buying fertilizers for their school flowers and plants, whether potted or not, schools can apply the tea and manures obtained from their worm farms. They are also good natural fertilizers for school gardens and farms. This also saves them a lot of money. Besides, worm manure and leachate are naturally produced plant nutrients and thus are more advantageous to use. If a school produces more manure in their worm farms than they will need, they can sell the rest to people that need it in order to make extra cash. Worms can also be sold to individuals and worm growers when their numbers increase greatly.

Learning opportunities for students
The ecosystem is an important topic in the curriculum of school systems across the globe. Experience has shown that students understand these topics easily and quickly when they are shown the specimen. Many schools organize excursions in worm farm facilities for their students as part of the study of the ecology of worms. Excursions are expensive projects, not just for the parents, but also for the schools and their teachers. But if there is a school farm, such excursion will no longer be necessary. During such lessons, students will simply move to the school farms with their teachers. Funds for the excursions can be diverted or used for excursions to other places.

Practical skills required for farm management
The school worm farms also give students the opportunity to learn how to establish and manage a worm farm in their various homes. As the need to save the atmosphere from decaying is becoming paramount, families and individuals are now encouraged to have worm farms in their various homes in order to reduce the amount of waste that goes into the landfill, which generates and emits a huge quantity of green gases into the atmosphere. Most children learn about worm farms and how to manage one in their schools and then introduce it in their homes. If they only gain theoretical knowledge

of such important projects in the schools, they will not have the required experience and practical skills to establish their worm farms in their home. It also helps students to develop into more responsible adults.

Going green
Green initiatives and campaigns are becoming stronger nowadays. Many people, institutions and organizations are now eco-friendly campaigners as a way of boosting their image among their customers and clients. A veritable means through which schools can identify with green campaigners is to go green. Parents who have tuned into the initiative are happy to send their kids to such schools. It is also a veritable means of getting grants from the government and funding from nongovernmental organizations that are interested in the campaign to save the atmosphere.

No danger involved
Worm farming is a completely risk-free enterprise that can be run in a school of any level. It exposes students to little or no danger. Decomposition of waste is achieved in a natural way. The compost does not generate any toxins or odor. So, even if schoolchildren go there without informing their teachers, they will not be exposed to any danger, physical or health wise. It is quite unlike the landfill which generates huge amount of methane and other green gases, which are not good for human inhalation. It also does not expose the school building and environment to any danger. Instead, it helps them to reduce costs and manage their waste in the most efficient manner.

From the above, you can see why it is important for school management to establish worm farms. Apart from the schoolchildren, the entire society will benefit from such a venture because it helps to reduce the quantity of waste that goes into the landfill on a daily basis and makes its management very easy, cheaper and more affordable.

Children and Worm Management
Worm farming may be somewhat challenging but not a task that cannot be accomplished by children. With the right instructions and proper supervision, children can manage their own or their family's

worm farms. If your child has an interest in vermiculture, you should not discourage him or her, rather, you should help the child to establish and run a robust worm farm. You can also ignite the interest in your child. The first thing you should do to help your child to develop interest in worm farming is to purchase a children's worm farming book for them and also a worm farm toy for them. As they read their book and play with their toy, it is likely that they will long to establish their own worm farm. Also teach them composting games. Many people don't know about compost related card games.

A typical example of such a game is the famed compost gin. The games are not difficult to learn. There are also websites that provide vermiculture pictures that children can colour which also helps them to learn about this natural means of making manure. Compost-related puzzles and compost word searches are also available online. Some sites provide such games free of charge. You should purchase such games for them and also sign them up in sites that offer it free.

Also teach your kids the basics of worm farming. Take time to learn the art yourself as explained in this book so that you will be able to teach your child. There are a lot of myths and false information surrounding worm farming which may frighten children and discourage them from building a vermicompost in their home. Clear their minds of these falsehoods and unfounded stories and teach them the truth about this type of farming. Let them know what they stand to gain if they have a worm farm of their own. By knowing the advantages of vermicompost and vermiculture, they will likely develop interest in such an enterprise.

Purchase the required equipment for the establishment and running of worm farms. Give them all the financial support they require in order to run a successful worm farm. You should also ensure that they apply all the necessary safety tips. Teach them the risks associated with worm farming and what to do to avoid being exposed to these risks. Ensure that they have their gloves. Don't allow them to do anything around the worm bin without wearing their gloves.

As a parent, if would be good to show an interest in worm farming and know how to run one to be able to teach a child.

Chapter 7. Worms and Ecological Sustainability

Earthworms are very important creatures on earth and they play some vital roles in the eco-system. Charles Darwin, after studying these wriggling creatures for sometime, declared that only a few animals have played roles in the history of the world as important as the roles played by worms; which he referred to as lowly organized creatures. Indeed, for many people these tiny creatures are despicable dirt creatures seen in the compost, under the earth or in any dirty environment. They regard them as creatures that have nothing to offer them.

This mind-set highlights the fact that many people do not know the importance of worm farming in the ecosystem. Though earthworms for many people don't have the excitement and charm evoked by other pets such as dogs and cats, their contribution to the ecosystem and sustenance of the ecosystem is inestimable. In this chapter, I am going to discuss the role of these tiny animals in the sustainability of the ecosystem, what feed on them and what they feed on. I will also suggest ways to protect them from their natural enemies, especially when they are kept in bins.

The Place of Worms in the Eco System

Worms have been useful to the world in which living things found themselves. Various studies carried out by evolutionists have shown that worms are among the first creatures on earth. Dinosaur waste was composted and transformed into a rich soil many years ago. Today, they still retain their title as the best composters ever. With their composting powers, they help in the sustenance of the atmosphere. We are all feeling the effect of global warming. But if mankind can farm these little creatures and deploy them for the processing of their waste, the amount of gas being released in the atmosphere will be reduced to a considerable extent.

Earthworms do not only process kitchen waste or food scraps, they also decompose animal dung and plant litter. If you have pets like a dog or cat, you can also establish a worm bin specifically for the decomposition of your pet's dung. You don't have to throw them inside your sewage system or dust bin. Just put them for your worms to turn into useful compost for you. They are also effective in recycling plant litter if you have them in your house. In this way, worms help to release the nutrients stored and locked in this animal dung to the soil to be fertilized.

When earthworms feed on these materials they release phosphorous and nitrogen in their casting and tea to the soil. Based on scientists' records, earthworm castings contains up to five times phosphorus than undigested soil. Besides, earthworms are able to absorb nutrients down through the soil profile and then take them to a level that is closer to the reach of the plant. In this way, plants are able to get more nutrients from the soil.

Worms' actions have a positive impact on the soil. Constant farming and other agricultural activities can also result in the depletion of nutrients in the soil. When the nutrients are used up by plants, agriculture will be affected. Mankind today has turned to inorganic fertilizers in order to increase the fertility of their soil and boost the harvest. But these fertilizers are like processed food that humans consume. Their use for farming can result in a lot of product but not without some terrible consequences to the consumers of this farm produce and also to agricultural land. Increase in cases of certain medical conditions is blamed for some of the chemicals used to boost harvest in agriculture.

This situation is worsened by civilization. Farmers do not have enough land for farming as more and more land is used for constructions of various kinds of facilities such as airports, stadiums, parks and the likes. These facilities are good but spell doom for the sustenance of agriculture as they require large areas of land.

Earthworms play a vital role in the sustenance of agriculture today. With worm castings and leachate which are naturally produced, rather than relying on inorganic fertilizers, farmers will increase the fertility of their land and get wonderful yields in a natural way. Crops and seeds produced with compost have no negative effect on any person that consumes them.

Apart from decomposing wastes and turning them into fertile soil, earthworms also till and aerate the soil when they are in the wild. As I have mentioned above in the classification of earthworm, a good species of these worms burrow vertically or horizontally, shallowly or deeply inside the earth. Air and water enter the earth through these channels and tunnels created by these tiny beings. With more water, air and holes in the earth, it will be very easy for farmers to till the soil. Plants' roots can easily penetrate the soil in search of food and the nutrients they require to grow very well. If they are able to absorb more nutrients, they will grow very well and yield more harvest.

Furthermore, earthworms are denominated ecosystem engineers because through their actions, they are able to positively alter the biological, chemical and physical properties of the profile of the soil. This change causes some rewarding effects on other organisms living within the soil ecosystem, influencing their activities and habitat.

Last but not least, earthworms are an essential part of the food chain on earth. A lot of animals feed on worms in order to survive. These creatures are not the most powerless. They also prey on certain microorganisms to survive.

From the above, you can see that these little creatures are not insignificant or abhorrent as some people may think. There is a need to accord them some respect they deserve. They are not just ordinary wriggling creatures found in dirt and rubbish heaps. They are working hard to save me and you, as well as our atmosphere and provide our plants with the nutrients they require to give us an abundant yield during harvest time. As Trish Fraser, an earthworm expert and a soil scientist will advise, you have to be gentle and affectionate with this great land tiller when next you see it struggling on the footpaths.

Also spare some thoughts to the multitude of earthworms toiling hard for us below the ground. If we can develop this attitude towards them, Fraser reasons that the important role they play in our lives will no longer be forgotten.

What Are Predators of Worms?

As has been said above, earthworms are a very important part of the food chain in the larger ecosystem. There are several other animals that prey on worms. Some other microorganisms are either in symbiotic or parasitic relationship with earthworms. If you are going to farm worms, it is of crucial importance that you know these predators so that you know what to do in order to avoid them. I have already mentioned some of these problems in a subheading of a previous chapter where we discussed earthworm concerns. So, as you read this, take what was said about some of these concerns into consideration here.

Certain actions of man

Man does not feed on earthworms but may be tagged the chief killer of earthworms. Some actions of man result in the death of millions of earthworms. Though earthworms are friends to farmers, farmers through the user of certain agricultural practices kill a lot of worms in their farms. Some of the chemically produced fertilizers used by some farmers to increase the fertility of their soil and boost harvest destroy earthworms and certain living organisms that live underneath the earth. Fertilisers contain salt, which not only burns these helpless creatures alive but also makes their natural home uninhabitable or unfavourable for their dwelling. Worms are also affected by rototilling and other mechanical means of ploughing the soil. So, if you are a farmer, consider these tiny creatures when deciding on the most suitable agricultural practices to use. In order to avoid the killing of earthworms inadvertently, establish a worm farm or vermicompost which will produce leachate and worm casting for you. They are very rich fertilizers and have little or no side effect on the environment and your crops.

Many leisure anglers and even some professional fishermen use earthworms as bait. You can imagine the number of earthworms that are killed on a daily basis by anglers during the summer period if you think of the number of holidaymakers and leisure seekers that go for pleasure fishing. This highlights the importance of worm farming. Without worm farming as a practice, earthworms would have gone into extinction given the rate at which they are killed and used as bait for fish.

Birds

Earthworms make a perfect meal for certain species of birds such as American robins, European robins, gulls, thrushes and starlings. Domestic fowls also eat worms. They go about scavenging for these wriggling creatures. However, birds, including fowl, do not constitute many problems to worm growers, especially worm farmers that keep their farms in a secure and shaded location in their home. These birds are not easily seen around human habitation areas unless in areas with vegetation. Besides, the worms are safe if their bins are lidded. So, if fowl or birds are seen scavenging within your locality, it is advisable that you keep your bins secure and protected from these predators.

Mammals

Worms in the food chain are also good meals for some mammals such as bears, pigs, moles, hedgehogs, foxes and others. These predators, with the exception of domesticated pigs, live in the wild. It is abnormal to see them around the human habitations. What to do depends on where you are living. Foxes for example, can be seen hunting at night in the countryside. So, if you are living in a location where these mammals hunt at night, you should be very careful with your worm bins.

Reptiles and amphibians

Some reptiles and amphibians such as lizards, snakes and toads also feed on worms. Certain species of lizards forage close to human homes. They are normally seen around the dumping grounds. So, if such reptiles are seen in your location, ensure that your worms are safe from their attack.

Invertebrates

Snails, slugs and beetles, especially ground beetles, enjoy earthworms as well. But it is almost impossible for these invertebrate to gain access to a well-protected worm bin.

Internal parasites

Microorganisms that have a parasitic relationship with earthworms are nematodes, platyhelminthes and protozoa. They live and obtain their nourishment from the intestines of worms. There are also some that are seen in the seminal vesicles, blood and coelon of worms.

Earthworms' cocoons are also not free from the attack of these parasites.

Now that you know the various predators of earthworms, the next thing to tell you is how you can protect and secure your worms against these natural enemies.

Note that natural predators are not only animals that feed on worms but also those that steal their food from them or that kill them to occupy their homes. Most invertebrates are in this class of predators.

How to Keep Your Worm Safe From Predators

Here are things that you should do in order to protect your worms from predators including those that eat their food.

• Ensure that your worm farm has the best conditions. Remove their leachate as instructed above so that there will be no odor from it which will attract certain predators like insects, flies and ants. Prepare the bed to maintain the suggested moisture level.

• Bury your worms' food inside the bed. This will keep away flies and insects as most of them cannot burrow.

• If you have poultry in your home, there is no problem with that. But keep your worm farm in a separate place or where your birds cannot get at it.

• Human beings don't feed on worms but there are cases of growers losing their worms to thieves. If you are living in a densely populated area, you should consider adding protection for your worms against human thieves. You may consider putting them in a shed with lock so that unwanted people will not have any access to them.

• Don't give them food that will attract pets like dogs. Dogs are also good scavengers. They like certain foods such as meat, fish, sausages and the likes. Only a well-trained dog can resist the temptation of hunting for leftovers. So, to save your dog from such temptation, it is advisable that you don't feed your worms with foods that dogs like. If you must provide them with such foods, then you have to also bury the food in the bin. Also avoid foods that can attract flies easily.

•It is also advisable that you cover your bin regularly or when you are not available to look after your worms. During hot weather, when it may be necessary to keep worm farm open for more fresh air to enter and to induce evaporation of more water, it is advisable that you keep your bin in a protected and shaded location such as garage where some of these natural predators cannot access.

Chapter 8. General Information about Worm Keeping

In the preceding chapters, we have dealt with worm farming basics. However, there are other important points that you should know, such as the equipment you will need to get started, what you should do and what you should avoid as a worm farmer, worm farming resources such as websites to purchase the tools you will need and online forums on worm farming to join. In this 8th chapter of this book, I am going to discuss them briefly so that you will be properly guided when it is time for you to start your own worm farm.

Worm Farming Dos and Don'ts

• Provide your worms with a variety of food in order to improve the quality of their castings and also to make them more robust. Give them a mix of brown and greens. The greens are rich in nitrogen while the browns are rich in carbon. Food considered as greens are coffee grounds, plant waste, crushed egg shells, veggie peels, tea leaves and cores. Those considered as browns are egg cartons, shredded newspaper and cardboard. With a meal plan that consists of nitrogen and carbon, your worms will produce leachate and casting that are highly rich in nutrients for plants and flowers. Do increase the quantity of browns you give to them when their bedding becomes more moistened than it should be. They are normally absorbent.

• Note that worms are picky and fragile. So, do not make their bins a dumping ground for all unwanted organic waste. Don't add foil, plastic, glass, polythene materials and any other items that are not biodegradable or items that can pierce their fragile bodies. Be observant as you feed your worms in order to find out the foods that they like eating quickly and the ones that they don't like. This will also help you to know what you should include in their meal plan. If you want to add new food, do that in moderation in the beginning to know whether or not your worms will like them.

• Don't use onion, garlic or citrus to prepare a staple for your worms.

- Be patient with your worms.

- Do join online forums on worm farming. You will learn a lot from the forum members. If you have any concerns, post it on the forum that you belong to.

- Don't build your worm farm with any material. Many people don't see any problem using a container made from metal as worm farm. Indeed, your worms may survive in them. But the reason why I advise against that is because of the high possibility of the metal rusting and leaking contaminants to the worm beds, which can be detrimental to the health of your worms. To forestall such an occurrence, you should consider using plastic and wooden containers. Plastic containers seem to be the best as it can be used in any location.

- Don't keep your worm bins close to a heat source. Light from the source will distract them and if it is very intense, it will burn them alive.

- Don't let your worms be exposed to air. Worms need oxygen to survive but it has to be in their natural home. One of the ways of exposing worms to air is to count your worms. Many people do count their worms when they receive them to find out if they receive the exact number they ordered. This may seem to be a wise decision but in reality, it is not a good practice. You don't have to count your worms to the last individual in the package unless they are very small in number (cupped bait). As you are counting them, you are exposing them to air and light. You may not know why worms hide under their bedding. Air and light dry them out quickly. When they are dried out, they die. To prevent the occurrence of such an ugly incident, they hide under the bedding. So, when you expose them, you facilitate their death. Some people will argue that they have counted thousands of worms and they did not die. They will not die right away if they are left exposed for a short period of time. But such exposure can stress them and make them sick.

- The best way to know whether your worms are all there or not is to weigh them. I have already mentioned above that worms are sold in pounds. Reweigh the package to find out if its poundage is what you ordered. But the package weight does not have to be exactly the same as stipulated in your order. This is because while in transit, the worms would have lost some water. Thus the weight can reduce but the difference will not be much. So, when you reweigh it and its weight is almost the same as your order, take it that your worms are all there. You don't have to recount them one by one.

• However, if you really want to recount them, then you should make an effort to limit exposure to light and air. The best way to do this is to first prepare their bedding. As you take them from the package one after the other, drop them directly to the bedding you prepare. It is also advisable to do this in a shaded space with minimal exposure to air and light. After counting the worms, spray some non-chlorinated water on them to moisten them and help them to recover the moisture they have lost.

• Keep only farmable species in bins. If you try to hold species that cannot be farmed in captivity, you may be wasting your time as they may not survive it. Unless you are a professional and experienced worm grower and you are able to differentiate various species of worms, you don't have to be moving about in the wild to dig up earthworms. The best practice for beginners is to order from a worm farm or online because it is difficult to differentiate worm species. They have similar characteristics. Difference in colour is not a sufficient sign of differences.

• When you receive your worms from the dealer, don't leave them in the package for days before transferring them to their homes. The package is meant to be their homes while they are in transit. They are not supposed remain there for a long time. If you are not going to transfer them immediately for one reason or the other, you have to keep them in a cool place. But on no account should you leave them there for more than two days; else, the next time you check on them, you are likely to find many of them dead or weak.

• Aerate your bedding at least once in a weak. Use a trowel to lift the bedding. Before you aerate, ensure that the worms have consumed the foods you provide them with. You can add more food after aeration. If you aerate when there is still food on the bedding, you can push it to the side where you don't keep food.

- Don't buy worms to put in your garden unless you have a properly moist and mulched garden, else they will all die sooner or later. Similarly, you cannot add worms to fresh compost. It has to be moistened, aged and turned before you can add worms to it.

Worm Farming and Vermicomposting Equipment You May Need

It is quite simple to start a worm farm because not much in terms of equipment is required to establish one. The basic things worms require to survive in captivity are food, proper environmental conditions and shelter, all of which we have discussed above in detail. However, there are certain equipment, tools and clothes that you may have to purchase in order to make the task simpler for you and also to protect yourself against any form of infection. Some of these tools are also suitable for composting and gardening. Here are the tools that you will require.

Glove: ideally, you need a pair of gloves to cover your hands when handling worm castings, worm juice and any organic waste to forestall the possibility of contracting infections.

Compost accelerator: As implicit from the name, a compost accelerator refers to any added feature to your worm bin in order to facility the activities of microbes in your worm farms. If the microbes are very active, it will take a lesser time for your worms to turn waste into a finished product or manure. Compost accelerator is important for people into vermicomposting. You can include this in your worm farm at any particular time that you want in the life of your worms. This is the major difference between a compost accelerator and a composter starter, which is normally added at the beginning of worm farming. Note that the inclusion of a compost accelerator in your worm farm will not make up for poorly prepared worm beds.

Compost activator or starter: If you are building a new worm farm or worm compost, you may consider adding a compost activator, which you will use to introduce microorganisms to your vermicompost.

Compost thermometer: You need a compost thermometer to take a measurement of the temperature of your bin or compost to ensure that it is within the range mentioned above. Ordinary thermometers used in measuring the human body's temperature is not a good fit to be used in a worm bin.

Compost sifter: This is also known as a compost screen used to get rid of unwanted materials from the compost. They are available in various sizes and designs and are sold in gardening stores.

Compost mixer: Also called a compost aerator, this tool, as the name suggests, is designed to turn up the bedding and compost in order to make it more aerated or to increase airflow in it. Though, such task can be accomplished with some other tools, a compost mixer makes it much easier, convenient and faster.

Compost grinder: You will require this tool if you have a very big worm farm. With the tool, the task of cutting and breaking your worms' food into tiny pieces to obtain a larger surface area will easily be achieved. The food scraps will be softer which will make it easier for your worms to work on them.

Compost turner: This is another tool that you will require if you are into a large scale composting. It is normally available in three types, namely, self-propelled, pull-type and front mounted. It is their method of operation that makes the difference.

Compost spreader: When you have finally made your compost and you want to spread it on your garden or farm in order to increase its fertility, you don't have to do that manually. You can save yourself from stress by using a compost spreader. It is designed to be able to spread compost on the garden or farm.

Trowel: Trowel can be used for a number of purposes in worm farming. You can use it to turn bedding. It is also the right tool to be used when you are preparing and laying bedding materials. The trowel also comes in handy during meal time. You can use it to collect and bury food scraps beneath the bedding for your worm's nourishment. Depending on the size of your worm bin, you may use the trowel when harvesting your worms, removing the casting and clearing old bedding.

Worm calculator: This is one of the innovations in the worm business. The tool is designed to help worm farmers to answer questions about their worms' population growth, financial value and vermicomposting capacity. Some of the models support 8 different currencies, metric and imperial metrics. It is a good tool for any person that will want to go into the worm business.

Bucket: You will require a bucket or any suitable container to collect the worm juice. Buckets are available in different sizes. The size to use depends on the size of your bin and the quantity of liquid produced by your worms.

Moisture meter: The moisture meter, as the name suggests, is used to measure the level of moisture in the bedding of a worm farm. It is an important tool, especially for beginners and people that don't know how the moisture level of bedding should be or those that cannot perform the ordinary moisture test as explained above.

pH meter and litmus paper: This tool is used to determine the pH level of a bedding. It is also an important material given the fact that worms do not survive in an acidic environment and thus, there is a need to ensure that their bedding is always within the stipulated pH level. However, if you cannot afford this meter, you may consider using litmus paper to determine when your bedding has become acidic. But litmus paper can only tell you when a medium has become acidic and it will not tell you the degree of acidity of the medium. You can find that out by using pH meter.

Hand rake: It is used to stir compost for enhanced aeration. It is also a very suitable tool to use for the transfer of worms from one tray to another or from the shipment package to their real home.

Scraper: It is made to be used for the scraping of already produced casting and other material in the compost and the cleaning of the rotating cleaner. It makes the work very easy.
Certain tools are more suitable for commercial worm farming. Typical examples of such tools are an automated bagging machine, semi-permanent timber, permanent concrete beds, fork lift, propagation box racking system, propagation boxes, permanent concrete beds and others.

Chapter 9. Reaping the Benefits of Your Labour

Worm farming is a good business if you know what to do and how to go about it. Consider the number of people that go fishing during the holiday period or as a pass time activity. Another good number are going into worm farming and vermicompost and they all will require worms. Given that worm farming businesses are few in number, there is high demand for these creatures. You can see that you will make some money from it if you are able to do it very well. Proceeds from such businesses in some jurisdiction are taxable, depending on the amount. In this chapter of the book, I am going to provide you with tips on how to establish your worm business, how to harvest your worms, castings and leachate and also how you will sell them.

Dividing Your Worms

As mentioned above, when a colony of worms increase in population to the capacity of their bin, they will stop procreating as a means of reducing competition for food and increase the chances of survival for themselves. When you notice that your worms are no longer growing in population, you have to divide or split them so that they will keep growing. Splitting worms is a veritable means of enlarging the number of worms you have. But in case you don't want to establish a new worm farm, you still have a need to split your worms for optimal performance of your worm herd.

You should also split your worms even if you are growing your worms to manage your waste. This is because splitting them will make the bin less stuffy and more aerated. You can sell the worms you don't need or give them out to people that may require them. If you have an aged outdoor compost pile or well mulched moist garden bed, you can transfer the surplus worms in your bin to there.

Dividing your worms' population is not a difficult task but it is not something that you can do anyhow. You have to do it in the right manner if you don't want to stress your worms and cause them any damage. Here are tips to help you get started:

- Don't start until your worms have increased in population. Increase in population is a clear indication that they are well established in their bin. As a rule of the thumb, you don't split worms when they are not well established in their initial bin. Ideally, you have to wait until after 4 to 6 months. If everything is ok with your worms, after this duration in the bin, they are supposed to have doubled or tripled their size. You can consider splitting them.

- Ensure that your worm bin has the best condition and that it does not have any foul odor before you can split them. A bin with an awful odor has not got the best condition. So, you have to improve the condition of your worms' bin using the tips given above for the odor to dissipate. If you divide the worms without getting rid of the odor, the old bin will continue to smell. Chances that the new bin will smell are also high.

- Get your new bin ready. Refer to what has been said on how to prepare the bedding for new worms. But if you are not able to prepare the bedding by yourself, you can purchase worm farms with already made bedding. Check the sources given above, you will be able to find worm bins that will meet your budget and requirements.

- Divide the old bedding together with worms into two and transfer half to the new bin. You don't have to count the worms. Use your common sense and power of sight to divide the worms. It does not have to be a 50:50 division. The top three to four inches of the total depth of the old bin's bedding normally will have more worms. So, remove these parts and keep them in a suitable container. Empty the remaining content in a clean plastic container in order to clean up and prepare the old bedding. Put back what you have removed there and add more bedding to the old bin. If the new bin comes with bedding and the depth of the bedding is not sufficient after you have added the worms and half of the bedding from the old bin, you can add more bedding to increase it.

- Check the moist level. If it is not sufficient, sprinkle water on the bedding until it becomes properly damp but not soaked. You should also check the temperature, aeration and pH level to ensure that everything is ok in the new bin.

- You are done. Keep taking care of your old and new bins as instructed above. They will soon double their population. Split again to keep your business moving.

Harvesting and Grading Worms: Tip

The harvest time is a period that every worm grower looks forward to. It is the time you will start to reap from the fruit of your effort. Harvesting of worms and splitting of worms are quite similar, except that harvesting also extends to removal of the casting and leachate. Worms produce a lot of casting which is their pool. Leaving it there for a long time is not good for the worms. It pollutes their environment. It is advisable that you harvest your worms and remove the casting at least once every three months to create a more favourable condition for your worms. There is the tendency for some people to think that their worms have not produced enough castings to be harvested because they feel that their worm bins' bedding has not increased in depth significantly. Normally, the bedding does not increase in depth even though you provide your worms food as and when due. It may even become lower than it was before. This is because the worms also consume the bedding.

To find out when there is enough casting in your bin, just scoop the layer of your bedding. The material underneath that looks like dark soil is the casting also known as vermin cast. The presence of this material tells you that it is time to harvest.

Earthworm harvesting is not difficult. Fortunately, there are different methods that can be used to achieve this. So, if one does not work for you, use another. Improvement in worm farming science and technology has also resulted in the fabrication of earthworm harvesting machines, which are available in different specifications and price ranges. If you can afford one, it is more practical to use it as it makes harvesting much easier. However, it is more of an option for a person into commercial worm farming. Here are various methods to apply for the harvesting. I would have talked about how to harvest the cast and worms differently but since in almost all the methods, the worms are normally separated from the cast, there is no need to separate them as it will amount to repetition.

Sifting method

This is one of the simplest methods to use. All you need is a worm sifter. Place some quantity of bedding from your bin into the sifter. Shake it gently for the cast to fall out. The worms and other undigested materials will remain on top. It will be easy for you to remove the undigested materials with your hands. Only the worms will remain now. I will tell you how to package the worms and what to do with the casting later.

Table harvesting

What you will need to harvest your worms in this method is just a table or board to be kept across or close to the worm-bed frame. A waterproof plastic material will be used to cover it. You will also require a container or more depending on the number of worms that you are expecting to harvest. It is in this container that you will keep the harvested worms in. Place about two inches of pre-soaked peat moss at the base of each of the containers that you will be using for this purpose. Scoop about 3 to 4 inches of bedding and put them on the table or board using a pitch fork. This entire process should take place in a bright or light environment. This will make the worms quickly burrow inside the peat moss once they are transferred. This method should be used if harvesting is carried out for the purpose of establishing a new worm farm as described above.

Hand method

In this method, you don't require any tools at all. You only need your hands and a pair of gloves. Use your hand to dig deep inside the bedding and collect a handful of compost and bedding material. Put it inside a tray. If you need the worms to start a new bin, prepare the bin and place all you have collected inside it. You can also dig in a couple of times to get the required number of worms. If you need the casting, remove the worms and take the casting.

Pyramid method

You will require a tarp to harvest worms using this method. The harvesting has to be done under sunlight. It is a method to use when almost everything inside the bin has been turned into casting, meaning that the bedding has to be consumed as well. Empty the contents of the entire bin inside a tarp which is spread under the sun. Create pyramids with the contents on the tarp. The worms will ordinarily move downwards and towards the middle to protect themselves from the effect of sunlight. Gradually be removing the casting away from the pyramid. When you get close to where the worms are, they will move close to the centre so that they sun will not affect them. Keep removing the casting until you get to a point where the worms have no hiding place. Quickly take the worms inside a bin and sprinkle water on them. Take the casting to your farm or wherever it is needed. If you are using this method, you should be wary of too much exposure to sunlight. You have to be fast in moving the worms to a protected place. If you cannot stay under sunlight, you can also improvise with artificial light. Just place the tarp under a shining light bulb or any light source.

Migration method
This method can be used when almost all bedding has been turned into vermicompost. Bring all the processed materials and the worms hiding inside them to one side of the bin and leave the other side empty. Fill the empty side with new bedding and keep your worms' food there. The majority of the worms will sense the food on the bedding and they will move there to feed themselves. So, after a couple of weeks, remove the old bedding. It may still contain some worms. You can sift it to get the remaining worms. The only problem with this method is that it will give you the castings and not the worms. Consequently, it is not a suitable method for growers that want both the casting and worms.

Corralling methods
This is also another method that you can use to harvest only the casting. You need to create a corral using burlap. You can also make use of a potato or onion bag that has holes. Prepare some bedding. Mix them with food and then put the mixture inside the bag. Bury it inside your worm bin or worm farm. You can also place it in the bin. The size of the bag to be used should be commensurable with the size of your bin. Don't add any more food to your worms in the bin. Within a couple of weeks, the worms will sense the food. They will move inside the bag. Bring out the bag and you have your casting. Empty the content of the bag inside a worm bin for the worms and continue to take care of your worms.

Cylinder spinning harvester

As already mentioned above, using machines is an option for people that are into commercial growing. You don't have to waste your money purchasing one if you have just a couple of bins for the processing of your kitchen waste or household organic waste. You can make do with the other methods explained above. But if you have enough money, it's worth buying. ¼ inch hardware cloth used to make the cylinder. The worm compost containing the worms is put inside it through the top. The machine spins the cylinder for the worm castings to be sifted out from the screen of the harvester. The worms and bigger particles will be brought out through the opening at the back of the machine.

Flow through bin

It is a special type of bin with harvesting features included underneath it. The composting worms occupy the upper chamber of the bin while the worm casting is thrown out of the container through the grate-like the bottom part of the upper bin. The bin is not spun. The castings just drop down as the worms move about because they are finer than the bedding and food substances. But when you want to ensure that all particles are pushed out, you can turn the bedding using a hand cultivator. If you have the money, you can purchase this type of bin rather than using household container as your bin.

The next thing to do after harvesting your worms and castings is to sell them.

Beginning a Worm Farm Business

If you have harvested plenty of worms and castings, you can sell them to make some money. But the big concern here is how to sell them and make money from them. With the right sales approach, you will be able to quickly sell and make money from your worm farm because many people need worms either for fishing or for the management and processing of their household organic waste into compost. Just like any other business, without adequate planning and strategizing, the business will not grow and therefore will not yield any profit.

The first thing you should do is to take time and learn about the nitty-gritty of the worm business. Some of the things that you should learn are who your customers are, where to find them, the suppliers, marketing strategies, how worms are graded and counted and packaging and storing of worms. Let me explain these basics one after the other.

Your target customers
- Anglers (both those that engage in it as a leisure and those that engage it for commercial purposes)
- Farmers, gardeners and composters (Farmers and individuals that are into composting and vermicomposting as well as households that want to establish worm bins to process their domestic waste)
- Fishing companies
- Worm farming retail stores and suppliers
- Fishing clubs

Where to find them
- Summer camps and parks with a fishable lake, ponds, river and water bodies
- Marinas
- Park offices, fishing access points and stores
- Farmer's and grower's residence and agro-base establishments

You will find a big market for your worms by the time you are able to find all the above mentioned establishments, individuals and organizations.

Worm Grading Systems
Another important aspect of worm farming business that you should be conversant with is the grading and counting systems of worms. As I mentioned above, worms are normally sold per weight and not by their numbers. However, there are some dealers that sell per count. Per count is usually used when only a small number of worms are to be sold as cupped bait. But large numbers of worms are sold per weight because of the reasons mentioned above.

Worms are also graded. There are basically two methods of grading worms. The first grading method is known as bait-size worms. In this grading method, bigger size of worms used as baits are packaged together. Worms that qualify for this grading system should be up to 2 inches long with a diameter of at least 1/8 inch. If you are planning to sell bait worms, then you have to take the pain to select worms that meet the requirements. There is a machine that does that. However, without this machine, you will still be able to pick them by hand. But you should avoid over exposing your worms to the sun. The second method of grading worms is known as bed-run. In this grading system, worms of all sizes are normally put together in a package. It is a good option for people that want to purchase worms to keep in bins.

What determines the grading and counting method to be used is your market or the people that you will be selling to. If you will be selling to anglers and other people that will be using the worms as bait, then you will have to sell cupped baits. But if you will be selling to growers, farmers, gardeners and individuals that want to establish worm farms, then you have to grade in bed-run. The same factor will also determine how you will weigh your worms. There are two methods of weighing, namely, hand counting and scaling. In hand counting, which is the traditional way of measuring worms to sell to anglers and fishermen, you hand count the worms and sell according to the number of worms in a package. The disadvantage of this method is that it is time consuming and can also result in the death of your worms. This is why many people nowadays prefer the second option, which is scaling. In this method, what matters is the weight of the packages and not actually the number of worms they contain. They will not contain the same number of worms but they will all have the same weight. This method is simpler and also reduces the exposure of worms to air and light.

Packaging your worms for shipping
This is a crucial aspect of the worm business and it has to be properly done, otherwise your worms will not get to their final destination. There are several packaging methods and containers used by worm dealers for the packaging and selling of their worms. To save yourself from the stress involved and the risk of the worms dying on the way as a result of poor packaging, you may consider using special worm packaging containers. The containers are available in different sizes. They can be purchased from earthworm wholesaling companies as well as suppliers and dealers. You can

also shop for them on online retail establishments such as eBay and Amazon. Normally, wax-coated cardboard or plastic is used to make the container because their ability to retain moisture is high. Besides, earthworms cannot eat them as they have no teeth. The containers have tiny holes for proper air circulation. The package should be properly labelled and held with shipping tape. The label must indicate that they contain live earthworms and should carry the warning that they should be handled with care and not exposed to extreme heat or cold. All should be written in bold letters. Some containers are made to contain 1,000 worms. But there are bigger ones that accommodate 1,500 and 2,000 worms.

However, if you cannot purchase the containers, you will still be able to ship your worms to their owners using other packaging methods. Get cardboard and line it with some newspaper and put down some bedding depending on the weight of the worms to be shipped. Take the worms and roll the newspaper over the top and seal up the cardboard. When they become hungry, they will consume the bedding. Note that a plastic container may not be a suitable container to ship worms because unlike the cardboard, it is not breathable. Besides, cardboard is insulating and when it gets to the final destination, the owner can also use it as part of the bedding by placing the container directly inside his own worm bin. You can also use a milk container for shipping. Just put a small quantity of bedding and keep them there. They will also enter inside. But this method is suitable for bait worms. Two heavy duty grocery bags joined together, stapled and lined in a small cardboard box will also work fine.

Note that shipping does not subject worms to stress. Many people erroneously think that worms die when they are shipped. This is far from the truth. It is only poor packaging and insufficient and improper shipping bedding that bring about the death of worms during shipping. However, this does not suggest that poor handling by shippers will not result in the death of worms. But cases of poor handling resulting in the death of worms are few. Another misconception about worm shipping is that worms cannot be shipped to a long distant location. With a proper shipper and vessel, worms can stay up to one month in transit. But for such long journey, it is good to provide them with enough bedding which they will feed on when they become hungry. If the total duration of the journey is about 10 days, you don't have to bother about providing them with extra food. Worms can live up to 10 days without food.

If you are shipping bagged worms, especially red worms, you will be very careful with the moisture level of the bedding. If the bedding is soaked, extreme temperatures will have different devastating effects on the worms. In the event of hot weather, the moisture will turn into steam that will cook the worms. On the other hand, if the weather is too cold, the moisture will turn to ice, which will freeze the worms to death. So, it is advisable that you provide little moist for your worms for such method of packaging worms.

Methods of Selling

You can sell your worms either through the conventional methods or online. If you want to sell online, you will need a web shop or you have to join an online market place such as eBay, Amazon and others. Take time to read easy methods of promoting and selling things online. In the conventional methods, you can sell to people directly from your worm farm. You will also have to take your worms for sale to farmers' markets, marinas, fishing access points, parks, beaches and similar places for people that are looking for bait to purchase from you. You should also identify some shops and suppliers of worms and worm farming tools and meet them to discuss the possibility of supplying them with worms and castings if they will need that.

Every successful business normally engages in one type of advert or the other. So, you should also find means of promoting your business. Join online forums. Put up adverts in your local newspaper. Use social media and have a blog where you will promote your business. You can also locally advertise your business by yourself by letting friends, relatives, colleagues and your neighbours know about your business. If you are able to popularize your business, locals that require worms will definitely come to you.

Doing proper advertising, at least within your locality, is of crucial importance especially if you are going to sell your worm casting and worm tea as well. This is because they are not good materials for shipping because of their weight. It will cost you a lot to ship them and the buyers may not be willing to pay such a high amount to get these rich plant nutrients. Most gardeners and farmers simply purchase from their neighbourhood or from any grower within their locality rather than paying for the high shipping cost. However, this does not mean that it cannot be shipped. All you need is to keep the right bags for them and securely tie them inside. You will definitely find a shipper that will be willing to ship them for you.

Costs to Consider

Before fixing your worms' price, it is important that you consider certain little expenses you will incur. These expenses may seem very little, but if you don't take them into consideration, they will add up to a large amount and may make you run some losses. Some of the expenses to consider include the delivery cost, cost for supplies (such as boxes, breathable bags and others), shipping cost and others. You should keep record of these costs before you fix the price of your worms otherwise, you are most likely going to run some losses.

Using Your Worms' Excreta

If you are growing worms just to manage your organic waste, it is of crucial importance that you know how to utilize your worms' excreta, otherwise they will also constitute some problems to you. The worm juice and cast are a highly rich source of nutrients to plants. So, the best thing to do with them is to utilize them in your garden to add more nutrients to your plants and vegetables. It can also be used to manure garden grasses so that they will be greener. They are a good source of nutrients for potted flowers and plants. You can use them in farms as well. There are no rules as to how to apply them. Just spread the casting and juice so that they will get to all angles of your garden or so that all plants and vegetables will get some share.

How to Prepare a Worm Casting Tea

Worm castings can be used to prepare rich tea for plants. There are different ways through which that can be achieved. But I am going to teach you the simplest form. Just collect a small quantity of castings and put it inside a bucket. The size of the bucket will depend on the quantity of castings collected. A five gallon (22.73

UK L or 18.93 US L) bucket will be enough for a small quantity of casting. Fill the bucket with water and leave the casting inside the bucket to be properly soaked with water overnight. The following day, the colour of the mixture will have a brownish colour.

You can use the liquid to water your plants and vegetables in your garden. But you have to first of all dilute it with water in the ratio of 1(worm tea):3(water). Don't allow the tea to sit for more than 48 days before using it.

Worm Farm Costs

As mentioned above, worm farming is not an expensive project to start. With a budget of $1,000 (£778.1) you can start a worm farm, even though the total amount required to set up one depends on the size of worm farm you want. Here are the possible worm farm costs:

- Average start-up cost: $250 to $1,000 (£194.53 - £778.1)

- Average yearly earnings: $15,000 – $15,000 (£11,671.5 - £11,6715) (depending on the quantity of worms and castings produced)

- Dirt/worm bedding: $80 (£62.25)

- Feeding: $100(£77.81) (more, less or none depending on the amount waste you generate from home and the number of your worms)

- Worms: 1kg of live red wriggler worms: $65 (£50.58) to $75 (£58.36)

1000 red wriggler worms = $25 (£19.45) - $30(£23.34)
One pound of European Nightcrawlers: $29(£22.56) – $30(£23.34)

Product	Description	Cost
Eco Classique Deluxe Worm Farm	Dimension: 65cm x 40cmx60cm (25.59inchesx15.75inchesx23.63inches) Features: a lid, 2 working trays, a reservoir, user manual, blankets, beddings, tea stimulator and 150 grams (5.29ounces) of worms	$90 (£70.03)
New Eco Classique 60 Litre Barrel Worm Farm	Height: waist height. Features: tea stimulator, user manual, bedding, blanket and 400 grams (14.11ounce) worms	$120 (£93.37)
Fibre Glass Bath	Two sided tarpaulin, 1 kilo (2.204 pounds) of Eisenia Fetida Worms, bedding, blanket, tea stimulator, bricks of finely chopped coconut fibre	$221 (£171.96)
New – Eco Classique Family Worm Farm	Dimension: 1.2M x0.6cmWx1MH (3ft 11.24inx1ft 11.62inx3ft 3.37) It comes with 500 grams (17.64ounce) of Eisenia fetida composting worms and two sided tarpaulin	$221 (£171.96)
Large Wooden Worm Farms	Dimension: 1.8mx1.2m (5ft 10.867inx3ft 11.24in) Features: tea activator, bedding, two sided tarpaulin,	$671 (£522.11)
Eco Classique Jumbo Wooden Worm Farm	Features: tea activator, user manual/instructions, felt cover, tarpaulin and 2 kilos (4.409) compost worms	$370 (£287.9)
Worm Factory 360 Farm Compost/Vermicompost Bin	Feature: soil pH level tester, moisture content sensor,	$134 (£104.27)
Worm farm factory composter composting compost bin + Kit	Made from bucket	$43.99 (£34.23)
Worm factory 360 farm compost vermicompost bin	Dimension: 18inchs x 18inches Features: Made from recycled plastic, lid, four stacking trays, legs of 22 inches (1ft 10in) high, instructions	$69.00 (£53.69)
Worm farming thermometer for composting bins	8 inches (0ft 8in) probe, color-coded gauge alerts, temperature accuracy range of 32 to 125degree F (0 to 51.67 degree Celsius	$15.95 (£12.41)

Product	Description	Cost
Worm Farm Compost Bin Moisture Content Sensor and Soil pH Balance Level Tester	Easy-to-read gauge, 9 inches (22.86cm) probes, no batteries required	$26.95 (£20.97)
Organic worm bedding for wormery – reptile bedding	Add water to expand to 10 litres (351.951UK fl oz), pH level of 5.7 – 6.8, odourless,	$9.08 (£7.07)
Worm Factory Refill Package	4 packages of 2 cup pumice, 4 jars of 8 ounce (0.237L) of mineral rock dust, 4 bricks of 250g (8.82oz) bricks of coconut coir	$19.95 (£15.52)
Compost accelerator 34 Oz	3x4.5x10 inches (7.62x11.43x25cm), 2.5 pounds (40.0ouces)	$16.99 (£13.22)
Gloves		$0.1 to $10 (£0.08 to £7.78)
Compost sifter		$30 to$40 (£23.34 to £31.12)
Compost mixer and aerator		$30-$70 (£23.34 to £54.47)

Note that each of these products has different designs, models and types. They also differ in their quality. So, their prices vary according to their type, quality, design and sizes. The prices given above are not fixed. You can find cheaper and more expensive ones.

Worm Farming Web Stores

Note: at the time of printing, all these websites fully functioning. As the internet changes rapidly, some sites might no longer be live when you read this book. That is, of course, out of our control

Whether you want to purchase worms or any particular worm farming tools, there are a lot of online stores where you will be able to purchase all the tools that you will require in order to establish a commercial vermicompost as well as small worm farm in your home or in your office. Here are some of the sites selling worm farming tools:

https://www.planetnatural.com
https://www.amazon.com
www.happydranch.com
www.wyndywoodwormfarm.com
www.worm-farm.co.za
www.farms.com
http://www.thewormfarm.net
https://unclejimswormfarm.com
http://www.gardeners.com
http://www.wormsdownunder.com

Worm Farming Forum to Join
One of the best means of obtaining reliable and concrete information and helpful tips on worm farming is to join worm forums.

Here are some of the forums on worm farming that you should join.
http://www.wormfarmingsecrets.com
https://permies.com
https://thefarmingforum.co.uk
https://www.daleysfruit.com.au
http://www.essentialbaby.com.au
http://www.caudata.org
www.wormman.com
http://forum.openbugfarm.com

Glossary

A
Acidity: The acid level of a medium, substance or environment (it can also refer to quality or state of being acidic.
Aeration: The process or act of circulating air in a worm bin
Aerobic: A condition that requires oxygen to occur or exist
Alkalinity: The state of being alkaline or the alkaline level of a medium, environment or substance
Anaerobic: A condition that does not require oxygen to occur or exist

B
Bait worms: (Also known as fishing bait) worms use to lure fish or any other animals to a hook.
Bedding: It is a medium provided to worms in the bins to serve as their living and resting place.
Bins: The container where worm farming activities take place. It is the housing system of worms.
Browns: Feedstock that is rich in carbon

C
Casting: Worm's excreta
Cocoon: the eggs of worms (egg capsules)
Compost: The processed waste used as manure for plants (composting can also refer to the process of producing compost)
Composter: A compost bin or a bin in which compost is produced
Compost tea: A mixture of compost or worm casting and water (it is also known as worm tea when it is prepared with worm casting)
Compostable material: Organic material that is turned into compost in a compost bin or worm bin by worms
Critters: Micro or macro organisms that feed and process compost material and organic waste into compost.

D
Decay: To decompose, go bad, rot

Decomposition: It is the process through which organic waste are broken down

Detritivorous: Living thing that feeds on plant and animal waste or trash such as wood lice

E
Ecosystem: A system formed by an ecological community and its environment which work together as a unit; it can also refer to as interconnectedness of organisms including microbes, animals and plants.

Egg casing: It is also the egg capsule of worms

F
Fertilizer: It is any substance that is rich in plant nutrient used to make the soil more fertile; it can be artificially produced or naturally made

Fishing bait: Worm or any other thing use to lure fish to the hook

Food scraps: Leftover foods that will be used as foods for the worms

G
Geophages: Animals that feed on humus soil which contains certain amount of organic content (typical example of such animals are earthworms, termites and others)

Greens: Foods that are rich in nitrogen

H
Heap: compost pile in an open place

Hermaphrodite: an animal that have both male and female genitals

Humus: Processed compost made from the decomposition of animal and plants waste which is very rich in plant nutrients

L
Leachate: Liquid generated in the worm bin as organic wastes are broken down. It is rich in plant nutrients. It is also referred to as worm juice by some people.

Leaf Mold: Almost decomposed leaves

Lime: a compound chemically composed of Calcium Carbonate or formalized as $CaCO_3$. It can be obtained from eggshell, sea shells, marble and limestone

M

Macroorganisms: Living organisms that can be seen with the naked eyes

Microbes: Microorganisms especially harmful bacteria (they can only be seen with a microscope)

Mulch: shredded and partially decomposed vegetable matter sprayed on top of beds and around the plants for protection, insulation, moist retention and weed elimination. It can also be sprayed for decorative purposes.

O

Organic waste: Organic material given to worms to process or turn into compost. It is unwanted biodegradable materials.

Overload: Putting a lot of foods into your worm bin to be aerobically processed

P

pH Value: it is a scientific measurement scale that ranges from 1 to 14 used to determine the degree of acidity/alkalinity of a substance. A pH value of 7 is a balanced or neutral value. Values lower than 7 are acidic and degree of acidity depends on small they are in the scale. Similarly, values higher than 7 are alkaline and the degree of alkalinity depends on how higher they are.

R

Rodent resistant bin: It is a type of bin made and equipped with features that will prevent rodents from building their home there.

Screening: To remove unprocessed materials from humus in order to obtain finer compost.

S

Soil conditioner: Any substance or material applied to the soil in order to boost its physical condition.

Stacked tire worm farm: a traditional method of growing worms for fishing, it is especially constructed on smallholdings and agricultural farms.

V

Vermi: Normally prefixed to culture (vermiculture) and compost (vermicompost) to mean worm farming and worm compost respectively, it is a Latin worm which means worm. It can also be prefixed to tea as in vermitea to mean worm tea.

Vermicompost: The act of processing compost with worms. It could also refer to a finished product of worm farm

Vermicomposter: A person that runs worm compost, or a worm bin

Vermiculture: An act of farming worms with the aim of obtaining worms to be used as bait or processing of organic waste

Vermitea: it is a term for the leachate produced in worm farm as food scraps are decomposed. It is also the liquid excreta of worms mixed with liquid from decaying waste material.

W

Worm bin/container: It is a container with bedding which serves as the housing system of worms when they are held in captivity

Worm farm: It is a set up where worms are grown either for their casting or to increase their population. Worms can also be grown there in order to process organic waste

Worm castings: The finished product of a worm farm consisting of worms' poop. It is rich in plant nutrients and thus used to improve the fertility of the soil.

Wet Garbage: It is compostable organic waste which includes garden waste, grass clippings and food scraps.